Praise for *TAKE A SHOT!*

"Take a Shot! is a fast and furious ride. It's *Moneyball*
meets *The Hangover!* I love it almost as much
as my Oscar and Lombardi Trophies."

— **Steve Tisch**, Chairman, New York Giants &
Academy Award–winning producer, *Forrest Gump*

"Insightful, funny, and full of great anecdotes, *Take a Shot!*
is a roller-coaster ride of a story. Jake reminds me of
Indiana Jones, never giving up until he reaches his goal."

— **Frank Marshall**, filmmaker

"Just like my start-up experience at ESPN and
the NFL Network, *Take a Shot!* captures the humor
and drive it takes to succeed against all odds."

— **Steve Bornstein**, EVP of Media, NFL &
President/CEO of the NFL Network

"The book is fast-paced and exciting. Jake's tenacity
is an inspiration to any entrepreneur, whatever the field.
And to think that this is only the beginning for Major League
Lacrosse is amazing. Could it be the next NFL? With Jake
and Dave at the helm, nothing would surprise me."

— **Doug Ellin**, creator and executive producer of HBO's *Entourage*

TAKE A SHOT!

ALSO BY JAKE STEINFELD

BODY BY JAKE: The Don't Quit Exercise Program

*DON'T QUIT!: Motivation and Exercise to Bring Out
the Winner in You—One Day at a Time*

*GET STRONG!: Body by Jake's Guide to Building Confidence,
Muscles, and a Great Future for Teenage Guys*

POWERLIVING BY JAKE: 11 Lessons to Change Your Life

*I'VE SEEN A LOT OF FAMOUS PEOPLE NAKED,
AND THEY'VE GOT NOTHING ON YOU!:
Business Secrets from the Ultimate Street-Smart Entrepreneur*

TAKE A SHOT!

A Remarkable Story of Perseverance, Friendship, and a Really Crazy Adventure

JAKE STEINFELD
and
DAVE MORROW

HAY HOUSE, INC.
Carlsbad, California • New York City
London • Sydney • Johannesburg
Vancouver • Hong Kong • New Delhi

Library of Congress Cataloging-in-Publication Data

Steinfeld, Jake.
   Take a shot! : a remarkable story of perseverance, friendship, and a really crazy ad-
venture / Jake Steinfeld, Dave Morrow.
      p. cm.
   ISBN 978-1-4019-4027-0 (hardback)
   1. Steinfeld, Jake. 2. Personal trainers--United States--Biography. 3. Actors--United
States--Biography. I. Morrow, Dave. II. Title.
   GV428.7.S84 2012
   613.7'1092--dc23
   [B]
                                                        2012013048

Hardcover ISBN: 978-1-4019-4027-0
Digital ISBN: 978-1-4019-4028-7

15 14 13 12   4 3 2 1
1st edition, August 2012

Printed in the United States of America

JAKE STEINFELD

For Tracey.
You give me the comfort of letting me do what
I do every day, always knowing you're by my side.

And for my kids, Morgan, Nick, Zach, and Luke.
I try my hardest every single day to make sure I leave
this place better than I found it—because of you.

DAVE MORROW

For my parents, Kevin and Renee Morrow.
You gave me so much and made
me the man I am today.

And for my lovely wife, Christine; and our
children, Samantha, Kevin, Jessica, and Maximus.
You all make me feel like there's nothing I can't do.

JAKE AND DAVE

For Jim and Anne Davis. Thank you for believing.

PREFACE

Have I got a story for you.

You like action? Suspense? Thrills? How about hairpin twists? Unforgettable characters? We've got 'em all. Or maybe you like stories about sports, or business, or heartwarming friendships? Check, check, and check.

But if what you really love is a good adventure—well, then, you're reading the right book.

This is a story about how three of the unlikeliest partners you'll ever meet—a shy Ivy League lacrosse star; the son of a famous TV evangelist; and me, the "Body by Jake" guy—decided to chase a crazy dream and wound up on the most remarkable journey of our lives. It's about how we broke all the rules and beat all the odds and never gave up . . . even when the walls were crashing down around us.

It's about the incredible things that can happen when you *take a shot*.

So buckle up, because you're in for the ride of your life. And wear something waterproof, because this adventure begins with a Category 3 hurricane.

○

The winds are howling at 50 mph. The rain is pouring down like an open faucet. Big trees are bending sideways like twigs. Any sane person has long since boarded up their windows and battened down the hatches. Hurricane Irene is pounding the Eastern Seaboard like a heavyweight boxer.

And what are we doing?

We're outside playing lacrosse.

We're in Annapolis, Maryland, and it's championship weekend for Major League Lacrosse. MLL, a professional outdoor lacrosse league that is currently wrapping up its 11th season—something *nobody* believed would ever happen—is about to hold a play-off game that will lead to the crowning of the league's 2011 champion. For days before these games, ticket sales were brisk, the media buzz was growing, and interest in the league was at an all-time high.

It looked like nothing short of an act of God could stop us now.

Then Irene showed up.

We started hearing news reports about a massive storm building strength and barreling up the East Coast. If you looked at a weather map of the U.S., you saw a huge, swirling ball of wind and rain that looked like a giant Pac-Man about to devour ten states—including Maryland. The Baltimore Orioles cancelled a doubleheader with the New York Yankees, and even the President of the United States warned the nation about "an extremely dangerous" weather event heading our way.

Then the mayor of Annapolis declared a full-blown state of emergency.

That's right, the mayor of the town where we were playing our games basically told people they'd be nuts to leave their homes.

So what did we do?

We said, "Let's play some lacrosse."

Don't get me wrong—we didn't just recklessly decide to stage our championship weekend in the middle of a hurricane.

We sat down and had a serious talk about our options. Look, we're not the NFL—not yet anyway—and we didn't have the luxury of moving games from one day to the next. If we didn't play today, we couldn't guarantee the availability of the stadium or even the players. If we postponed the games, we might have to cancel them altogether. We ran the risk of having a permanent asterisk in our records books.

We could end up a league without a champion in 2011.

At the same time, we obviously didn't want to endanger anyone. But the weather radar didn't show any lightning, and that's what worried us the most—after all, we couldn't have our players running around with titanium sticks acting like human lighting rods. But fierce rain and ferocious winds? We felt we could handle those.

In other words, if you think a little hurricane was going to stop us, you don't know Jake.

Fortunately, Navy-Marine Corps Memorial Stadium was privately owned and couldn't be shut down by city officials. ESPN2, the sports network providing TV coverage of the games, told us that if we stuck it out, they would, too. Our players, not surprisingly, were ready to roll. The rest of the Eastern Seaboard was boarding up and burrowing in, but for Major League Lacrosse, it was showtime.

An hour before the play-off game, the winds and rain really picked up. The new synthetic turf at Navy-Marine Corps Memorial Stadium got so saturated that our players looked like guys jogging through a flooded basement. Our longtime MLL announcers, Joe Beninati and Quint Kessenich, told our TV audience that there were "columns of rain coming down" in what amounted to "car-wash conditions." They weren't exaggerating. I sat in a suite along with my wife, Tracey; my three sons; and MLL Commissioner Dave Gross, wondering if we'd soon see Dorothy's house fly by.

But then something amazing happened.

The guys started playing awesome lacrosse.

Right in the middle of this hellacious storm, we watched the greatest lacrosse players in the world do what they do best. The Hamilton Nationals and the Denver Outlaws were putting on a big-time show. Great passes, incredible goals, nonstop action—the few hundred die-hard fans wrapped in yellow slickers and clutching inverted umbrellas got to witness some of the best lacrosse I've ever seen.

And then the rain let up a little, and for the first time all afternoon I began to think that we would be okay.

And that's when Irene, the wench, turned ugly.

Suddenly the rain was coming down like Niagara Falls. The players looked like they were wading in the Amazon. The goalposts on the football field we were playing on were swaying so hard they looked like they were going to get sucked into the sky. We had sponsor signage boards all around the field, and they were popping off their hinges and threatening to become deadly projectiles.

I sat there fearing for the safety of the fans, the players, and, yes, the Denver Outlawettes—six cheerleaders in shorts, cowboy boots, and hopelessly ruined mascara (talk about guts—these gals were doing kicks and splits in the middle of a typhoon!).

With the sky darkening and the winds howling, I knew what we had to do.

I turned to our commissioner and said, "Dave, we gotta shut this down."

○

So what happened? Did we call off the game and end our season on a soggy note?

Are you kidding?

With Dave Gross and me on the verge of stopping the action, Tracey calmly turned to us and said, "Just give it a minute. Maybe it'll let up." That's my wife for you—cool as a cucumber. So we sat there, waiting and praying while the apocalypse unfolded around us. The stadium was rattling like it was made out of tin. I'm telling you, that minute felt like ten hours. Could we really hope the worst storm in a decade would suddenly just "let up"?

But then, wouldn't you know it, it did.

The rains eased up a tiny bit. The winds went from howling to just plain nasty. No patio furniture flew by our booth. So we made sure our signage boards were taken down and our cheerleaders were out of harm's way, and we kept playing.

We played straight through Hurricane Irene.

Toward the end of the game, one of the biggest stars Major League Lacrosse has ever known, Casey Powell, scored on a beautiful diving shot.

His team, the Hamilton Nationals, beat the Denver Outlaws 11 to 9 and advanced to the championship game.

And the next day, in *perfect* weather, the Boston Cannons—who had won the earlier play-off game—beat Hamilton to win the championship and take home the coveted Steinfeld Cup.

We dubbed the play-offs "the Hurricane Games," and ESPN loved that so much they replayed the games the next weekend and made them part of their collection for ESPN Classic. The NFL had its Ice Bowl—MLL now had the Hurricane Games.

Nothing stops Major League Lacrosse, baby!

Then again, the fact that we're even here today is a miracle.

Because the real story of Major League Lacrosse is about how close it came to never happening at all.

Trust me, all the catastrophes, complications, and craziness I'm about to describe to you make Hurricane Irene look like a gentle sea breeze.

INTRODUCTION

The weekend of the Hurricane Games was truly incredible, and the way we played through one hell of a storm says a lot about our league.

But this book isn't about Major League Lacrosse in 2011.

No, it's about an even crazier time in MLL's history—the three insane years, from the summer of 1998 to the summer of 2001, that It took to get the league off the ground.

It's the story of how the three of us—Dave Morrow, an introverted kid from Detroit who started a lacrosse company out of his Princeton dorm room; Tim Robertson, the son of TV evangelist Pat Robertson and a successful media mogul in his own right; and me, Jake Steinfeld, who you might know as Body by Jake—joined forces to start a pro sports league, even though we didn't have any real idea how to do it. (Hey, who does? Leagues don't come in a box with instructions.)

It's about how the three of us shared a goal of creating something that didn't exist before: a league where the world's best players could play—and where kids with tiny lacrosse sticks in their hands could hope to be stars someday. We knew if we could somehow pull it off, we wouldn't only be fulfilling our dream—we'd be creating the opportunity for thousands of other dreams to come true, too.

But beyond the story of our partnership, this book also tells the tale of how the ultimate "fish out of water" (that would be Dave) hooked up with the ultimate showman (that would be me) and learned a few lessons along the way—and how Dave turned around and taught me a few as well. Dave and I couldn't have been more different, but we set out on our voyage with only a handshake deal, and we stayed side by side through every step of our unpredictable adventure.

And now we're doing something we've talked about doing for a long time—we are telling our story. For years people have come up and asked us how this adventure really unfolded, so we finally want to set the record straight. You'll notice this book is in both my and Dave's voices, as it should be. Tim Robertson was an equal partner, but it was Dave and I who spent the most time together working on the day-to-day business of launching a league, and so we'll be the ones telling the story. Picture Dave and me hanging out at a party. You walk by, pull up a chair, and sit next to us. I lean over and start telling you this unbelievable story, and then I elbow Dave and say, "You tell 'em this part, buddy." Well, that's how this book is set up.

And while I'm sure our story will provide you with more than a few laughs at our expense, we hope this book does more than entertain you.

We hope it *inspires* you, too.

Because life is all about facing obstacles and finding a way under, over, around, or straight through them. Was Irene a particularly scary obstacle? You bet. But anyone who dares to dream will likely face a scary moment like that—a moment when your dreams seem to be dangling by a thread.

Hopefully, your own moment won't involve a Category 3 hurricane. But it probably will involve something that will knock you silly, kick you down, and push you to the brink of surrender. You know what, though? *Those* are the moments when you find out what you're made of.

This book is filled with moments like that.

And if Dave, Tim, and I could tackle such a long-shot challenge and somehow come out smiling, we hope you realize that there isn't any dream too crazy to come true.

Of course, we can't tell you how to make your dream a reality. We barely knew what we were doing with ours.

But we can tell you what you absolutely *must* do to have any chance of succeeding.

You have to get up, get out there, and take a shot.

That's exactly what we did on our amazing adventure. We got in the game. We bet on ourselves. We never quit. *We took a shot.*

And to think the whole thing started so innocently, with me locked in a workout duel with one of the most famous guys on the planet.

It is May 1998, and I am running like a maniac around the grounds of a luxury hotel in Detroit, Michigan.

I'm in the middle of a three-mile sprint that my workout partner has referred to as "a little jog," and I'm digging down deep just to keep up with this guy, who runs strongly and effortlessly and is in *phenomenal* shape. Now listen, I'm in pretty good shape myself. But the thing is, I'm not a big fan of running. In the sixth grade, I did manage to finish the 50-yard dash—in three days. So I'm not exactly Usain Bolt.

But here I am, sprinting around the hotel, trying to keep up with this gazelle I'm running with. This guy is barely breathing hard, so I hide my fatigue and keep going, too. There's no way I'm ever gonna let him see me struggle, even though I'm sweating like a farm animal. Just a day earlier, I had put him through my rigorous workout, and he did surprisingly well. I've seen a lot of people raise the white flag halfway through my routine, but not this guy. So I was going to keep up with him, even if it knocked me out. And around mile two, it looked like it might.

"Come on, Jake, we're almost finished," the guy says to me.

"No sweat," I say to J-Man—the nickname I've given to John F. Kennedy, Jr.

○

How did I end up in a fitness throwdown with the renowned son of a President? Me, someone who started life as a fat kid with zero confidence and a bad stutter?

Let me back up the story just a bit.

As a kid growing up in middle-class Baldwin, New York, I had some pretty serious confidence issues. In addition to being chubby, I stuttered so badly that I didn't like making phone calls, even to order pizza (and I loved pizza, which shows you how bad my stutter was). I might have stayed that way if my dad, a street-smart Navy veteran, hadn't come home one summer day with a set of weights and a weight bench. He put them in the backyard and said, "Let's go do some bench presses."

And since I was too busy eating a Twinkie or stuffing some other kind of junk food down my throat, I said, "No thanks, Dad."

So the bench and the weights stayed in the yard, unused, all summer. Then in the fall my father told me to bring them into the basement laundry room. It so happens my bedroom was in the basement, too. It was a pretty cool room, with a Jimi Hendrix poster on one wall and an Alice Cooper poster on another, and a desk where I did everything I could to avoid studying.

Well, one night I was dragging myself through some social-studies homework, and I leaned back in my chair and started daydreaming, as I often did, when I happened to notice a barbell sticking out of the laundry room.

Just because I was so bored with my homework, I got up and brought the bar into my bedroom. It was an E-Z curl bar, with not a whole lot of weight on it. I set up this long skinny mirror on top of my ottoman, and I put on a tank top to cover my belly. Then I went over to the turntable and put on a record. Did I choose Hendrix or Cooper or some headbanging heavy-metal song? Nah.

I put on Frank Sinatra.

That's right, I loved listening to Frank sing a live version of "My Way," not so much because of the song, but because, after he finished, there was a long burst of wild applause from the audience. And there was something about that applause that really fired me up. So I put on my headphones, stood in front of the mirror, and, with my gut hanging over my underpants, I lifted the curl bar for the first time.

That first curl was a magic moment in my life.

I started doing my bicep curls to the sound of that applause, imagining I was doing it in front of 50,000 screaming fans at Madison Square Garden with all those people cheering for me. The weights became my best friends, and the more muscular I got, the more my confidence and self-esteem grew. Over time, I even gained more control of my stutter. Then when the girls started to notice me, man, I was really over the moon.

Can you imagine what a powerful realization that was for me? That I didn't have to let the world tell me who or what I was—*that I could decide what the world believed about me?*

I got into great shape and never looked back. I started seeing thousands of people cheering me on no matter what I was doing. Even when I was mowing the lawn of our home, I'd visualize that I was actually mowing the outfield at Yankee Stadium. I'd even stop and wave to all the fans, acknowledging their cheers. My mom would look out the window, see me waving at imaginary people, and ask me what I was doing.

"Ma, I'm waving to the fans!" I'd say, "I'm in Yankee Stadium!"

And my mom would think, *What is wrong with that boy?*

○

My first serious dream in life was to become Mr. America. I bought bodybuilding magazines, watched every *Hercules* movie ever made, and even ordered exercise products from Charles Atlas. I got briefly sidetracked when I enrolled in State University of New York at Cortland in upstate New York, but I was so anxious to make my dream come true that I "retired" from college a few months into my freshman year. I moved to California when I was 19 with a few bucks my parents gave to me to rent an apartment and lease a Chevy Camaro.

I don't know if my folks believed I'd achieve my goal, but I do know they believed in me.

I was lucky enough to have someone else in my life who championed me from an early age: my wonderful, incredible grandmother Myra Duberstein. She was my go-to person—the person who always told me how special I was and how I could accomplish anything. She gave me permission to dream big. She believed in me so much that her confidence seeped into my system and stayed with me for the rest of my life. I don't know where I would have wound up without my Grandma Myra.

Before long, though, I had to readjust my goals. You see, all those weight-lifting magazines I read in my teens told me that if I ate 18 eggs and 24 chickens every day, I too could grow up to become Mr. America.

Well, I clucked a lot, but I didn't become Mr. America.

What I discovered after entering the Mr. Southern California bodybuilding contest (and coming in second) was that in order to compete professionally, you had to take steroids. And that just wasn't something I wanted to get into. But I loved working out, and I knew that whatever dream I chased next, it would have something to do with fitness.

Around that time, I got a request from a young actress who lived in my apartment complex in Studio City, California. She'd seen me hanging out by the pool, and she asked if I could help get her in top shape for a TV commercial in which she'd appear in a bikini.

"How much do you charge?" she asked me.

My standard fee back then was . . . I had no fee. I'd never trained anyone before. So I agreed to do it for gas money to her boyfriend's house.

Then she said, "I like you, Jake, but I don't want to *look* like you." Back in the early '80s, women were intimidated by using weights; they thought they'd end up with big, bulky muscles. So I improvised and used household items like a towel and a broomstick to do resistance training.

Well, it worked. This actress got in fantastic shape. When she went to Hollywood parties, people asked her how she'd done it, and she told them about me. When they asked her for my number, she couldn't give it to them, because it was unlisted. Not for any reason— it just was.

And that only made people want to find me even *more*.

It gave me a certain mystique—totally by accident, mind you. Everyone was saying, "You gotta get Jake."

Then someone gave a friend a training session with me as a birthday present. I went over to this guy's house in Beverly Hills, not sure of what to expect. I walked in and saw a thin guy with glasses who was wearing a T-shirt, gym shorts, and tennis shoes. He was nervous and looked like a kid on his way to a school-yard fight he wanted no part of.

"I haven't worked out since the eighth grade," he told me. "So go easy."

For the next 30 minutes, I put Steven Spielberg through his paces.

○

The director of *Jaws* and *E.T.* did a great job. Yet what struck me most about him was how warm and friendly he was. He was becoming a big deal in Hollywood and could have been standoffish or self-centered, but he was the opposite of that: he was a regular guy. And since I am the same way, Steven and I hit it off right away.

True, he called me an hour after that first workout and told me he couldn't move his legs or arms. "Is this normal?" he asked. "I think I'm partially paralyzed."

But he recovered just fine, and we formed a great friendship. I nicknamed him "Spiels," and then "Weils," because of the way the wheels in his head were always turning.

And in our time together, I began picking his brain so I could learn more about what made him tick. He was just really down-to-earth, like your buddy from the neighborhood, and I was smart enough to realize that there was a lot I could learn from him—lessons I could apply to my own life and journey. So I peppered him with questions, trying to glean some insight into his formula for success.

It was during one of our workout sessions at his beach home in Malibu that I asked Weils a simple question. At the time I'd developed a nice roster of celebrity clients—not only Weils, but Priscilla Presley, Harrison Ford, and Bette Midler, just to name a few. I became the "trainer to the stars," and even *People* magazine wrote a story about how I'd pioneered the personal-fitness-training industry.

But while I had a little dough in my pocket, I still had a long way to go, if you know what I mean. So that's why I asked Steven that simple question.

"Weils, what's it like to have money?"

He looked at me and gave a one-word answer.

"Freedom."

He then further explained that "Being successful allows you to do whatever you want to do, whenever you want to do it, with whomever you want to do it with."

Boy, did that sound good to me.

I knew I wasn't going to direct *E.T. 2*, but I believed I could be successful in the field I had chosen—fitness. So that became my one consuming goal. I incorporated my company under the name Body by Jake—a name I picked because I thought it sounded pretty smooth. Within a few years of my conversation with Weils about freedom, I'd become CEO of Body by Jake Enterprises, a multimedia product and marketing company. I developed fitness products and sold them through TV infomercials that made me pretty popular. Eventually, I created FitTV, the first 24-hour television network devoted exclusively to fitness; and I conceived and starred in my own Family Channel sitcom, *Big Brother Jake.*

Then, because I'd been such a fan of bodybuilding magazines growing up, I decided to create my own fitness and lifestyle magazine, *Body by Jake.*

And that brings me back to my workout challenge with the J-Man.

○

In 1998, I went to the biggest magazine publisher around— Hachette Filipacchi Media, publisher of *Elle, Woman's Day,* and a bunch of other titles—and told their CEO, David Pecker, about my idea for a magazine. I really liked David—he was a razor-sharp guy with tremendous energy. He got what I was trying to do with my magazine, and he agreed to back it. *Body by Jake* was in business.

To get things off the ground, I had to go out and personally drum up advertising pages—the lifeblood of any magazine. For me, that was no problem. I'm a natural salesman, so going out and doing what I call my "rap-a-doo" about fitness is my idea of a good time. I had recently read an article about an old friend of mine who'd become the chief marketing officer at Ford. I knew that securing advertising pages from Ford would give my new magazine a real boost, so I called and asked him if he could help.

"Jake, I've been on the job for all of seven days," he told me. "You've got to give me more time."

"You've had seven days," I told him. "I'll give you three more."

Then I had an idea. Hachette Filipacchi was publishing a hip new magazine called *Swing*, which was run by Ralph Lauren's son David. It was also publishing a high-profile political magazine launched by John F. Kennedy, Jr., called *George*. So I said, "If I can bring JFK, Jr., and David Lauren with me, will you see us?"

"If you can bring John Kennedy, Jr., with you, you're in."

"Done," I said.

Of course I had no idea if I could deliver.

So I called David Pecker, who put me in touch with John. We spoke on the phone, and I persuaded him to come with me to pitch Ford and General Motors for advertising pages. John and I got to know each other aboard Hachette's corporate jet on the flight to Detroit, and we hit it off immediately. Just like Weils, he was a regular, down-to-earth guy. We shared some stories and had some laughs, and up in that plane it was easy to forget that he was such a prominent guy.

But out in public, it was another story.

I guess I didn't quite understand the extent of his appeal until I got to hang out with him. I didn't realize how charismatic he was until I saw people's jaws literally drop when he walked by. I saw people walk into chairs when he was around—women *and* men. I realized right away that wherever we went together, all eyes would be on him.

We checked into our hotel in Detroit, and the next morning I asked John if he wanted to train with me.

"Sure, Jake, I'll work out with you," he said, "if you take a run with me later."

Like I said, I'm not a big fan of running, but I agreed. We went to the hotel gym, and John trained with me. We did my usual 42-minute, high-octane routine, with a series of 100-repetition sets and no resting in between. John huffed and puffed his way through set after set, but he never gave up. I have trained a lot of people who quit in the middle of this workout, but not J-Man. At the end of the session, he was beat, but he never stopped smiling.

That afternoon, John, David Lauren, and I had our first pitch meeting, at General Motors. As I expected, a roomful of hardened corporate executives collectively went gaga when John walked in. I could have been wearing my gold lamé posing trunks and no one would have given me a second look.

I was up first, so I gave my speech about *Body by Jake*, and I answered some tough questions about projected circulation and things like that. There were a lot of fitness publications on newsstands at the time, and the General Motors guys were really making me earn whatever I was going to hopefully get from them. But I felt it went pretty well.

Then it was J-Man's turn to pitch.

He got up from his chair . . . and everyone immediately applauded. He told a couple of stories and answered a couple of questions about what he did over the weekend. I mean, these guys were hanging on his every last word. And J-Man gave me a look as if to say, "That wasn't so hard, Jake, now was it?"

"Wait a minute," I said in mock exasperation, "you ask me about my circulation numbers, and you ask him how his weekend went?"

But, hey, that was John. He got a commitment for a bunch of advertising pages, and David and I got a couple, too.

We were all pumped up from the great pitch meeting when we got back to the hotel, and I wasn't really surprised when John said, "Okay, let's go for that run." I was hoping he might have forgotten our bargain, but he hadn't. I hemmed and hawed, but it was no use. I was going running with J-Man.

Halfway through our "jog" I was ready for smelling salts. When we finally stopped, John was slightly out of breath while I was trying not to wheeze too loud. He casually asked if I wanted to join him for a cup of coffee, and I politely said I wanted to go back to my room and get ready for our pitch meeting with Ford.

In fact, my legs were really stiffening up, and I knew if I didn't take a breather I'd have to go to that meeting with a walker.

○

In the end I made it to the meeting just fine without the walker, and John and I gave our pitches, got some ad pages, and took off to the airport.

Before boarding in Detroit, I said good-bye to John and David and wished them good luck with their magazines, and I got on a plane to take me back to Los Angeles. We had given each other a copy of our magazines, so on the flight home I started leafing through David Lauren's publication, *Swing.* I opened it up and saw a photo of a young guy holding a lacrosse stick, and I started reading the article. It was about a kid named Dave Morrow, who'd grown up in Detroit; played lacrosse at Princeton; and started Warrior, a lacrosse equipment company, out of his dorm room. The story described how Dave was changing the perception of lacrosse and turning it into a lifestyle.

Sitting in that plane 35,000 feet in the air, I thought to myself, *This kid is onto something.*

You see, I had a connection to lacrosse. Growing up on Long Island, I was a basketball guy at heart, but I also loved playing lacrosse. It had everything I liked: hitting, scoring, and speed. I played in high school as well as in my first and only semester at Cortland State. I was a decent player and pretty good at facing off. But other than that, I didn't see much playing time.

Then one November afternoon in my freshman year in college, we were scrimmaging at Syracuse University, a perennial lacrosse powerhouse, in the freezing rain. I remember coming off the soggy field after a face-off and standing on the sidelines and looking like a lacrosse ice sculpture. That's when I asked myself, *What am I doing here?*

I realized that playing lacrosse was kind of a dead end for me. There was no such thing as a professional outdoor lacrosse league. Remember how I imagined all those people cheering for me? Well, that wasn't going to happen with this particular sport. So I stopped playing and moved to California to pursue bodybuilding.

Yet when I read the article about Dave, I remembered how much fun playing lacrosse was, and I got all fired up about the sport again. And that's when a crazy idea popped in my head.

When I got back to L.A., I called David Lauren and got Dave Morrow's number. I tracked him down in his Warrior offices in suburban Detroit, and introduced myself.

"Hi, I'm Jake," I said, "from Body by Jake."

He didn't believe me for a second. He was sure it was one of his buddies playing a prank on him.

I eventually persuaded him it was me, and after a few minutes of conversation, I asked him one simple question.

"Dave, is there such a thing as professional outdoor lacrosse?"

Dave told me there wasn't.

The next three words out of my mouth changed both of our lives.

I said, "There is now."

○ ○ ○

2

You might be wondering why I would make such a bold statement, especially to someone I'd never even met.

Well, what can I tell you? It's just the way my brain works. Just because something doesn't exist, doesn't mean that it can't exist.

And it certainly doesn't mean I can't be the one to make it happen.

You see, everybody has dreams, and everybody comes up with good ideas—and some people come up with really amazing, kick-ass ideas. Then you go home at night and write down your kick-ass idea, and you're all fired up and convinced that you've found a way to change the world. You can't *wait* to start making it happen.

Then you do something that changes everything. You go to sleep.

You wake up in the morning, and all of a sudden that kick-ass idea you had the night before doesn't seem all that kick-ass anymore. And you start to think about the 150 reasons why that idea can't possibly work, and as fired up as you were the night before, that's how deflated you suddenly are in the light of day. By the time you've finished your breakfast, you've convinced yourself that your idea won't work. So you file the idea away, or maybe you forget it altogether.

Just like that, *you have stopped you.*

You didn't even give someone else a chance to stop you—you did it all by yourself. Unfortunately, that's what happens to most good ideas: they get snuffed out by the very people who have them.

I'm a little different when it comes to ideas. When I think of something that strikes me as promising, I don't file it away. I run with it, and I don't stop—ever. And I don't just take a few cautious steps to test the waters.

I go full speed right from the start.

Still, declaring I was going to start a pro lacrosse league? After only a few minutes on the phone with Dave?

The truth is, before reading that article and calling Dave, I had never even thought about starting a pro lacrosse league. It hadn't been the slightest blip on my radar. It just wasn't something I'd spent any time thinking about at all, and certainly not anything I ever seriously considered.

But at that time I definitely *was* in the market for a new goal. Remember I told you about how I started FitTV, the first 24-hour fitness-lifestyle television network? Well, I wound up selling the network to News Corp's Fox Networks Group for a really nice chunk of change. I'd been doing pretty well before then, but the sale bumped me up to a whole new level. It gave me that precious thing Weils and I had spoken about all those years earlier.

It gave me freedom.

So in 1998 I was looking around for a brand-new challenge. Back then, people in Hollywood were buying minor-league baseball teams. Snapping up a club like the Toledo Mud Hens was all the rage. I have to admit, I thought about it, if only because I had really enjoyed playing Little League as a kid. As a matter of fact, I pitched a four-hitter against Jewish war veterans when I was in the fifth grade (record keeping back then was pretty sketchy so you can't look it up, but my mom'll tell you it's true). Did I now want to be the owner of my own minor-league club?

The answer was no: I'm a Steinfeld, not a Steinbrenner.

So I was on the prowl for some new challenge when—*bam!*— I start leafing through *Swing* magazine on the plane. Funny how the universe works, right? But that's the thing about inspiration: you never know how or when it's going to hit you, so you always have to be prepared. Life is all about moments, and you have to be ready to seize your moment when it arrives.

That's why I called Dave Morrow.

It's a little something I've always done that I call "Dialing for Dollars." When I read about someone doing something that really fascinates me, I call and get the lowdown straight from the horse's mouth. CEOs, movie moguls, investment gurus—doesn't matter. I track them down, call them, and get right to it. To this day, I go through several newspapers every morning and clip out at least four or five articles with the names of people I want to reach out to. I can't tell you how many amazing people I've met because of those calls.

Dialing for Dollars, baby.

And Dave Morrow was one of those guys who jumped right off the page and got me to pick up the phone. The *Swing* article talked about how Dave was a former All-American player who started a lacrosse equipment company out of his dorm room at Princeton. About how he and his father developed a new titanium stick that was really starting to catch on in the lacrosse community. About how he was marketing lacrosse as a cool and youthful lifestyle sport, appealing to a whole new generation of players and fans. I liked his ambition and his moxie, but most of all I liked his approach to lacrosse.

Dave was taking the things I loved most about the sport—high-speed play, hard hitting, lots of scoring, lots of *action*—and putting them front and center.

So I tracked him down and made my pitch about a pro league.

Meanwhile, on the other end of the phone, Dave was wondering, *Who the hell is this guy?*

○

On the day Dave Morrow turned 13, his dad, Kevin, handed him a big cardboard box. Inside the box was an alarm clock; a pair of steel-toe work boots; and a blue polyester uniform, with the name Industrial Tool & Engineering stitched on one breast pocket, and Dave's name in a small white oval stitched on the other.

"Happy birthday, son," his dad told him. "You've got a job now."
That moment explains a lot about the kind of man Dave grew up to become.

Let's have Dave tell you more about himself:

My folks raised me in a middle-class neighborhood in Troy, Michigan. My dad owned a machine shop that remanufactured the systems used by the steel industry to make giant steel slabs. He was one of those guys who worked really hard and had a great mind for business; he never went to college but started his first business when he was 21, and he went on to create several different successful businesses, from a newspaper to an Irish pub. He pushed his kids to work hard, too, and that's why he recruited me to work in his factory when I turned 13—because he thought it would make a man out of me.

So at 5:15 every summer morning, I would hear that alarm clock ring and drag myself out of bed—if I didn't, my old man would come in and pull me out of bed by my ankles. And we would drive together to the factory on the corner of Plymouth and Schaefer, in a bombed-out, crime-ridden section of downtown Detroit.

My first job was cleaning the giant machines in the shop—big lathes that cut through steel and huge mills that shaped hard materials. I'd finish a day of work covered in oil and grease and tiny steel chips that got in my hair and skin. I worked alongside some tough characters: big, blue-collar guys from Russia and Poland who were missing fingers and had other gruesome injuries from years of factory work. I was a boy among men, and in my early days at the shop I was too intimidated to even go into the lunchroom and mingle with the greasy grizzly bears during breaks.

I kept to myself until the shop foreman told me I was making the men look bad by not taking breaks, and I had to go in and talk to them. Finally I did, and before too long I was just one of the guys.

It was many years later that I realized what that job did for me: It made *me* a tough character, too.

For one thing, it physically strengthened me more than any workout ever could. I was lifting steel bolts that were as long as bedposts and weighed 70 lbs., and I was handling jackhammers and big wrenches, so I developed the kind of total body strength some athletes only dream of.

But the job also made me tough inside—it taught me how to get things done. At the factory there weren't any performance plans or incentive reviews or any of that junk—there was just my dad screaming at his guys to gut it out, work the line, get it done. Consequently, I was physically and mentally stronger than most guys my age as I headed off to college.

Back then I loved to play hockey, and I had some colleges recruiting me for their squads. But I also loved playing lacrosse, and I was good enough to have Princeton—one of the very top universities in the country—interested in me. I was torn between playing hockey at a lesser college and playing lacrosse at Princeton. I asked my dad for advice, and in return he asked me one question.

"When you get out of college, would you rather play professional hockey or own a professional hockey team?"

"Own a team," I responded.

"Then go to Princeton," my father said, "because you'll meet the kind of guys who will help you fulfill that dream."

And that's what I did.

Princeton was my first experience as a fish out of water. It was full of trust-fund babies and kids whose parents and grandparents went there—and a few Rockefellers and Du Ponts to boot. On my first day there, some freshman asked me what prep school I had gone to.

I didn't even know what a prep school was.

So I hung out with other lacrosse players and had a pretty good time. The Princeton Tigers weren't exactly a lacrosse powerhouse; in fact, they had a 20-year streak of losing seasons. So they brought in players like me to turn the team around—not that anyone really believed we could do it.

It was in my junior year that I had the idea that changed my life. I was a pretty aggressive lacrosse player, and I was constantly bending and breaking my sticks. Originally, lacrosse sticks were made of wood, before giving way to low-grade aluminum. They were lightweight and inexpensive, but they bent all the time. Then one day, my dad and I were kicking around ideas for how to make a better stick. At the factory, we had built a durable synthetic snowshoe for a company called Atlas, and we had tested different materials, including aluminum and a much tougher metal, titanium.

"Why can't we make the lacrosse stick out of titanium?" I asked.

My dad and I churned out some primitive samples—really nothing more than long titanium tubes—and I handed them out to my Princeton teammates. The feedback was great: players loved the stick and loved that it didn't bend and break so easily.

Then in 1992, Princeton defeated Syracuse in the NCAA lacrosse finals, for the first NCAA lacrosse championship in our school's history.

And we did it using titanium handles that weren't even a commercial product yet.

College coaches started calling my dad at the factory. Our first product was a titanium handle that sold for $99 —a lot more than the $19 most aluminum handles cost. We sent a couple of sticks to almost every lacrosse coach in the country and told them that if they liked them they could pay for them and keep them; if they didn't, they could send them back.

Not a single coach sent them back. In fact, a lot of coaches bought them with their own credit cards.

Now we needed a name for our company. My high-school lacrosse team had been called the Warriors, and we thought that was perfect—it captured the primal nature of the game. So we became Warrior. Then we needed a slogan.

A two-man ad agency we hired came up with "The Means to Dominate." Pretty cool, huh?

When most of my Princeton classmates graduated, they went straight to big-money jobs on Wall Street. I went home and cranked out lacrosse sticks. Warrior had about $300,000 in sales its first year, but I only made around $20,000.

"Exactly why am I doing this?" I asked my dad.

"Don't worry about what everyone else is doing," he told me. "You'll be fine. It just takes time."

So I decided to stick it out.

And that's when Jake came into the picture.

3

When I called Dave, it wasn't at all clear that Warrior would ever make it big in the equipment industry. Dave was maxing out his credit cards—then getting creative on applications to get *more* cards—just to keep it all going.

That didn't matter to me.

Sure, Dave was definitely a little green around the gills. He hadn't traveled a lot or seen much of the world outside of New Jersey and Detroit. Besides getting married, he hadn't really changed all that much since his college days.

That didn't matter to me, either.

What mattered was what my gut was telling me about Dave.

It was telling me the kid was onto something. Dave was on the verge of taking lacrosse to the next level.

He was marketing lacrosse as a high-octane game that was anything but the stuffy, prep-school sport most people perceived it to be. Dave was tapping directly into the energy and excitement of a new breed of extreme sports—motocross, snowboarding, freestyle skiing, mountain biking—that was exploding in the 1990s.

As I read the article about him in *Swing*, it really got me excited about lacrosse all over again. And it really inspired me to want to talk to Dave and find out more about him.

So when I called, I peppered him with questions. I asked him if he had connections with the best lacrosse players. I asked him where Warrior's best markets were, and which parts of the country were up-and-coming. It quickly became obvious that this guy knew the sport inside out.

And that's when it occurred to me: Why mess around with a minor-league baseball team when you can create a pro outdoor lacrosse league?

I had a gut feeling about Dave Morrow as I was speaking with him, and for me, that's usually all I need. I trust my gut and I always have—that is my MO. And I've been right about people a whole lot more than I've been wrong.

So I never asked Dave for his résumé—a good thing, too, because he woudn't have had one typed up. I never worried that he was too young or inexperienced for this challenge. I just made up my mind that he was my guy, and I told him I would fly him out to meet me in Los Angeles so we could talk more about a pro lacrosse league.

Here's how Dave remembers our first meeting:

> When I got the message that Jake had called, I was pretty sure it was one of my college buddies pranking me. Even when I called the number back and got Jake's assistant, I almost hung up. I figured my buddy had got the real number and given it to me, just to bust my chops. Then the assistant put me through, and suddenly I was talking with Jake from Body by Jake. That was weird.
>
> But Jake is one of those guys who, in the first three minutes of talking with you, makes you feel like you've known him for ten years. He said he found out about me in *Swing* magazine and wanted me to come out to Los Angeles to talk about starting a professional outdoor lacrosse league. On his dime. I had a couple of pals who were living in Manhattan Beach, so I said, why not go out?

I told my parents about the call, and my dad immediately said, "Body by Jake? That bodybuilder? You know a lot of those bodybuilders are a little off, don't you? This guy just wants to get you alone and hit on you." I told my dad he didn't have to worry, and I flew off to L.A.

Jake had a car waiting for me at the airport—the first time I ever had a car waiting for me anywhere. He put me up at the Lowe's in Santa Monica, and when I got to my room I found a huge fruit basket waiting for me on the dining-room table. Muffins, cookies, everything, wrapped up like a giant Easter basket. First time anyone ever got me a fruit basket, too. Then I saw a message from Jake—he was switching the location of our meeting the next day from his office to his house.

I seriously began to wonder, *Was my dad right?*

When I got to Jake's house I immediately started looking around for signs that he wasn't, as my dad had put it, off. The first things I saw in the driveway were a basketball hoop and a couple of kids' bikes—two really good signs. Then his wife answered the door—a really great sign. Inside his house I saw a lot of photos of Jake with his wife and kids, and I finally began to relax.

Then Jake came out on crutches, with his foot in a big cast. His wife and two young kids were with him.

"Hey Dave, great to meet ya, buddy!" he said. "Sorry about doing this at the house, but as you can see I'm not very mobile right now. I blew out my Achilles tendon playing basketball."

We sat down and Jake started talking a mile a minute, like he does, telling me his whole story and pitching me on a pro lacrosse league. I'm from the Midwest and I wasn't used to people talking that fast, pitching ideas, doing what Jake calls his rap-a-doo. And I certainly didn't know anyone with famous Hollywood friends like Steven Spielberg and Harrison Ford. I didn't even know if I should believe Jake about all his famous friends. He may have sensed that, because at one point he picked up the phone and started dialing, saying, "You want me to call Spielberg? He's my buddy, I'll call him right now."

"Jake, no, I believe you," I said. "Hang up the phone."

That's Jake. He is this force of nature, and the way he works is that he breaks you down and knocks you off balance and does whatever it takes to win you over. I've seen him do that with big CEOs, guys who run billion-dollar companies—he'll go into a meeting and put them in a headlock and joke around with them like they're old pals. And Jake wins them all over. He's impossible to resist.

Look, Jake and I could not have been more different. He operates at this breakneck pace, and I'm really mellow —I move a lot slower than that. Jake loves being out front and onstage, and I hate that; I'd much rather be behind the scenes. Jake has this big, contagious personality, and he's a genius at promotion. And for me, the whole process of starting a league and being out front was a very unnatural process.

But it was obvious to me from that first meeting that Jake is a stand-up guy who means what he says. Do you know how rare a thing like that is? Lots of people tell you they're gonna do something, and then never follow up. Jake says he's going to do something, and he does it. Right in that first meeting, I felt I could completely trust him. So right then and there, we agreed to go forward with this crazy idea for a league.

So that's how Dave and I partnered up. A guy who's more amped up than the Energizer Bunny and a laid-back, long-haired kid barely out of college—neither one of whom had any idea of how to start a league.

Why would anyone doubt us?

In fact, the challenge we picked for ourselves could hardly have been more daunting.

We didn't know it going in, but within a few years of our decision to launch a league, a bunch of other pro sports leagues crashed and burned—and those were started by people who knew what they were doing!

World Wrestling Federation owner Vince McMahon announced that he was starting the XFL, a rebel professional football league that would play its games in the summer, the NFL's off-season. Millions and millions of dollars got pumped into the league, which finally debuted in 2001.

It shut down after just one season.

Some other guys had the idea to start a league for SlamBall—a version of basketball played on trampolines! They even got Philadelphia 76ers owner Pat Croce to sign on as an investor.

That league lasted two seasons.

Then there was the Women's United Soccer Association, which was born right after the U.S. women's soccer team shocked the world and created a national frenzy by beating China in the 1999 FIFA Women's World Cup (remember Brandi Chastain whipping her shirt off?).

The league signed up the 20 best female soccer players in the world, wrangled some huge investors, and launched with eight teams in April 2001. I remember being at their first game in RFK Stadium in Washington, D.C. I was there with my buddies Andy Heller from Turner Broadcasting System and Fred Dressler from Time Warner Cable (both companies had invested in WUSA). The league had a whole bunch of A-list investors and partners, including John Hendricks, who'd founded the Discovery Channel and had the idea to launch WUSA. The stadium was completely packed, and excitement about the league was stratospheric. No one in their right mind could have watched that game and believed the league would be anything but a big success.

It folded after three seasons.

So, yeah, starting a pro sports league was an incredible long shot. Thank goodness none of us consulted our crystal balls, because if we had, I doubt we would have gone forward.

Yet even without psychic ability, we had plenty of other reasons not to do this. For one thing, lacrosse wasn't exactly the world's most popular sport. So that was strike one. Launching a league usually takes tens of millions of dollars, and Dave and I sure didn't have that kind of dough. Strike two. And we had exactly zero years' experience in the world of pro sports leagues.

Strike three, we're out.

But hey, we're talking lacrosse, not baseball. So Dave and I agreed during that first meeting to take our shot.

In that meeting, I told Dave something that laid the foundation for our friendship, and for Major League Lacrosse: "Look, man, whatever craziness happens, *no matter what*, as long as we have each other's backs, we will be okay."

We shook hands, and that was that. No contract, no lawyers, no partnership agreement—just a handshake. To this day, that's all Dave and I have ever had—a handshake.

That is all two friends ever really need.

Even so, when I said, "whatever craziness happens," neither Dave nor I had any idea what kind of craziness lay ahead.

What I did know is that, once Dave was on board, I had to fill out the team. It was like I was putting a really great band together, and I had to bring in a couple of superstar musicians. A pro sports league would only be as strong as its partners, so it was crucial we recruit some heavy hitters for our adventure.

And I knew just the man for the job.

It was time for me to call Big T.

○ ○ ○

About ten years before I got the idea to start a pro lacrosse league, I had another off-the-charts brainstorm: to create a TV sitcom starring yours truly.

A fitness expert with very little acting experience and a serious Long Island accent starring in his own half-hour TV comedy . . . a no-brainer, right?

In fact, the idea wasn't as loopy as it might sound. This was the late 1980s, and I was on TV a lot in those days with my syndicated *Body by Jake* fitness show. I was pretty comfortable in front of an audience, and had been ever since my very first taste of showbiz—appearing onstage with the Village People.

That's right, I got approached by a Casablanca Records executive while I was buying vitamins in a drugstore in 1978, and next thing you know I'm onstage at the Santa Monica Civic Center flexing my muscles in front of tens of thousands of screaming fans, with the Village People singing their monster hit "Macho Man" behind me. Was it how I envisioned breaking into showbiz? Uh, not exactly.

But hey, everybody's got to start somewhere.

The point is, I could handle myself pretty well in front of an audience, so doing a scripted comedy show didn't seem all that daunting to me. So I pitched an idea to the guy running CBS Entertainment. It was called *Big Brother Jake,* and it was about how my character, a tough guy from Brooklyn named Jake—big stretch—wound up being a Big Brother to five foster kids. CBS loved the idea and signed on to do the show.

I was feeling pretty good about myself, having just inked a network sitcom deal, when I got ready to hop on a plane to Houston to attend the 1988 National Association of Television Program Executives (NATPE) convention. Just before I boarded my plane, I went to a pay phone and checked my messages (yes, there used to be pay phones back in the day).

The first message was someone telling me CBS had just fired the executive who green-lit my idea. Which meant my sitcom was out on its butt, too.

Bad news? Sure. But I didn't mope—I didn't have time. I had a job to do at the NATPE convention. I was there to renew and promote my *Body by Jake* TV show, and to sign T-shirts and shake hands. Now, at that moment it might have seemed like my dream of doing a sitcom could not have been deader. But that's the funny thing about dreams—you never know how close you are to having them come true. That's why you can never, ever give up on an idea that you're passionate about. Because your big break could be just around the corner.

Or in line waiting to have a T-shirt signed.

I was doing my thing when a guy who was in line with his children suddenly asked me, "Hey Jake, have you ever thought of doing a TV show with kids?"

I played it cool and said, "Sure, I've thought about it."

The guy then explained that his wife loved my fitness show—and that his kids learned to count while listening to me count off reps on the show. He said he was head of programming at a network called CBN, the Christian Broadcasting Network. He handed me his card and said I should call him.

But instead of taking his card, I gave him my number and told him to call me.

The truth is, I didn't really think twice about his offer. I had just had my sitcom shot down at CBS, one of the big three networks, so I didn't get all that excited about some network I'd never even heard of. I put it out of my mind and went about my business, and I figured if this guy was serious, he would call.

Well, he called.

Then he flew me out to the CBN campus in Virginia Beach, Virginia, to pitch my idea to network execs. I showed up for my 10 `A.M. meeting a little early, like I always do, and took a seat in the waiting area.

No sign of this guy.

It was 10:30. Then 11:00. And still—no guy.

I am never late for anything, so this was really making me nuts. I was sitting there thinking that I was being punked. At around 11:20, some other guy I hadn't met walked by the waiting area, looked at me, and said, "Hey, you're Body by Jake!"

"Yeah, how's it going?" I said.

"What are you doing here?" he asked. So I filled him in.

He probably felt bad that I had been waiting for an hour and a half, so he invited me to his office and said, "Why don't you tell me about your idea?" Well, that was all I needed to hear. My rule is, if you have an audience, tell 'em your story. I'll pitch anyone, anywhere, anytime. So I launched into my idea for *Big Brother Jake,* and when I was finished, the guy looked at me and said, "Sure, let's do it."

Just like that.

The guy's name was Tim Robertson, and he owned the network.

○

We did 100 episodes of *Big Brother Jake* on CBN, which eventually became the Family Channel. Along the way, Tim helped me launch FitTV, and gave me the chance to make two of my biggest dreams come true. But he gave me something that I cherish even more: his friendship.

Tim is just a really great and fascinating guy. His dad is Pat Robertson, who is probably the most famous and influential Christian minister in the country, as well as the founder of the Christian Broadcasting Network. Tim studied liberal arts at the University of Virginia, but from early on, he saw a future for himself in the communications industry. So he set about learning the business from the ground up. He got his first job when he was 16, as a CBN grip, or the guy who helps move scenery around. His salary was $1.65 an hour.

He went on to work nearly every job there is in broadcasting —hanging lights, audio engineering, field production, segment director, show producer. When his dad handed over the reins of CBN, Tim turned it into a cable powerhouse, rebranding it as the Family Channel and creating an impressive line of original shows— including mine.

Tim and I came from pretty different worlds, but in those early years of working together, we became great pals. Tim has four daughters and one son, and I remember giving his son, Willis, his first lacrosse stick when he was just a little kid. And get this: Willis went on to become a star player in high school.

I knew that although Tim hadn't played lacrosse growing up, he had a personal connection to the sport through his son. I also knew that if I could sell him on my idea for a professional league *and* tap into his expertise in media, it would be a huge boost for our team . . . which, at that point, was just Dave and me.

So I called Tim and told him all about Dave and Warrior and our idea for launching a league. I expected Tim to say what he had said when I pitched him in the past: "Sure, let's do it." Instead, he said, "You know, Jake, sports is a really tough business."

Okay, so Tim didn't just jump right in at first. But I got the sense that he wanted to be on board, and I was convinced he was the guy for us. One of the secrets to being successful in business is picking the right partners, and I was certain that Tim would be the perfect partner for Dave and me. Now, all I needed was something to tip him over the edge—something to sweep him up in the passion that Dave and I felt for lacrosse.

I had the perfect thing. Dave had mentioned that he would be playing on the U.S. national team competing in the 1998 Federation of International Lacrosse World Championship, which that year was being played in Baltimore, Maryland. This would be one of those rare times when all the best lacrosse players in the world got together in one place, and Dave invited me to come see him play for the American team.

What better way to symbolically kick off our pro lacrosse league than by watching the sport played at the highest level on the biggest stage?

Besides, the U.S. team hadn't lost a major world championship in decades—proof that the very best players on the planet were right here in our backyard. Watching another rousing American victory, which was all but guaranteed, would be the perfect way to light a fire under us all and generate some real heat for our prospective pro league. So I invited Tim to come watch the game, and we set out for Baltimore to cheer the U.S. team on to victory.

What could possibly go wrong?

○

Heading into the 1998 World Championships, Warrior, Dave's lacrosse equipment company, was still relatively small. They were moving a lot of sticks, but their sales weren't anywhere close to those of the big equipment companies.

In 1996, the International Lacrosse Federation offered an exclusive sponsorship deal for the '98 championships for the tidy sum of $150,000. Whichever company snagged it would get the exclusive rights to outfit the players and do on-site branding and capitalize on the games being on TV. For a company like Warrior, that kind of exposure was priceless.

Still, coming up with $150,000 was, for Dave, about as easy as playing lacrosse blindfolded. And besides, he figured that one of the two major equipment brands would snap up the rights.

Well, neither company did, assuming they'd swoop in and get at least half the business anyway without paying for a sponsorship. That gave Dave the chance to grab the exclusive deal—all he had to do was come up with $150,000.

Dave realized, and rightly so, that this was an opportunity he simply couldn't pass up. He had to find some way to come up with the cash.

He found it in his junk mail.

Specifically, he stopped throwing out all those solicitations for credit cards he got in the mail, and started filling them out instead. At the time Dave's new wife, Christine, a fellow Princeton alum and a geochemist by trade, was serving as Warrior's comptroller. Together they sat down and applied for a bunch of different cards. And they got a little creative when reporting Dave's income.

Then the credit cards started pouring in, one after another, until they had amassed about $250,000 in credit.

Dave used those cards to snap up the exclusive sponsorship deal for Warrior, but there was another problem.

At the time, Warrior had a small product line: a couple of sticks and a pair of gloves. Dave had bought a great platform to promote his equipment, but *he had nothing to promote.*

So as soon as he signed on the dotted line and forked over the big bucks, Dave got on a plane and flew to Asia to get some products made.

Was he a little unprepared for what he was doing? You could say that.

Dave got to China and drove to a factory in the middle of nowhere. Nothing but rice paddies and a dirt road. He sat down in a room full of factory managers with their notepads out, waiting for him to tell them what to do. He thought about what he was going to say, and he came up with nothing. So he told the truth.

"Look, fellas," he said, "I have no idea what I'm doing. I need you to teach me how this works."

Dave spent the next two weeks on the factory floor, going over different fabrics and samples and hammering out a line of lacrosse products. Once the factory managers showed him all the machines and what they could produce, Dave kicked into high gear. He had a background in manufacturing; he *understood* this stuff. Although he came to China with only a vague idea of the product line he wanted, he went home with a sparkling array of Warrior lacrosse equipment —arm pads, shoulder pads, chest pads, gloves, sticks, jerseys, you name it.

Warrior was ready for its close-up.

Now all Dave had to do was go out and win the championship.

I flew to Baltimore with my son Nick, who was five at the time but already playing lacrosse. We met up with Tim and his son, Willis, and sat in the stands of Homewood Field, the lacrosse stadium at Johns Hopkins University and one of the most hallowed fields in the sport. We sat with Dave's wife, Christine; his mother-in-law, Rose Marie; and a bunch of their friends, and settled in to watch the championship game, the U.S. against Canada. Thousands of fans were packed in the stands, and the place was crackling with excitement. And on the field, every U.S. player was decked out in Warrior gear and carrying a Warrior stick. The energy in Homewood Field was just amazing. It felt like something really incredible was about to happen.

Once the game got under way, boy, it didn't disappoint. Along with Dave, there were some incredible lacrosse players on the team, including Casey Powell and Mark Millon, probably the two best players in the world at that time. They played brilliantly, scoring some amazing goals. Dave himself was incredible. He was known as a disciplined, aggressive defender, and he was always given the assignment of shutting down the other team's leading scorer. And that's just what he did.

The U.S. jumped out to a big lead and was winning by ten goals— an absolutely insurmountable margin—with only 12 minutes to play. I sat in the stands nudging Tim, as if to say, "Ain't this great?"

Then Team Canada scored a goal.

Then they scored another one.

And another.

Hey, it was nothing to worry about—the U.S. team still had a big lead. But suddenly our guys were making sloppy plays. Missed checks, bad passes, lost face-offs. Canada kept scoring, and all of a sudden they were only two goals behind. With two minutes to play, a Team Canada player streaked toward the U.S. net. Dave Morrow overplayed him to one side, and the guy slipped underneath him, fired a shot, and scored. Canada now trailed by one.

Then, with 30 seconds, the impossible happened: Canada scored again and tied the game.

The U.S. team was now on the brink of an epic collapse.

Up in the stands, all those happy, excited fans were now biting their fingernails. Dave's mother-in-law couldn't even bear to watch, so she took my son and hid in the tunnel, waiting for the game to end.

Fortunately, Canada didn't score again in regulation. The game went into overtime.

On the sidelines, the general manager of the U.S. team pulled Dave aside. "The U.S. hasn't lost a major world championship in 30 years," he said. "If we lose this game, you're not gonna be able to *give* your Warrior stuff away."

Dave got the sickening feeling that his dream was slipping away.

It hadn't been an easy past few weeks for him. He was working like a madman to get his new Warrior products ready; during one stretch, he was away from home, and his new wife, for *35 straight weekends.* There were plenty of times his attention got pulled away from practicing by some emergency at Warrior. Often he'd be running onto the field right before a game and get a message that an order had gotten screwed up.

Dave was under an *enormous* amount of pressure to launch Warrior, and even more pressure to win the championship. And now he was losing it.

The U.S. and Canada were still tied at the end of overtime, so the game went into double OT. Talk about nerve-racking. It was almost midnight. The stands were in a frenzy. I could only imagine what Dave must have been feeling down on the field. His team, and his dream, were on the very edge of disaster.

Could somebody please score a goal and win this thing?

Then, late in the second overtime, Mark Millon swooped in, reared back, took a mighty shot . . . and scored.

The U.S. won the game!

The fans went *nuts*. Tim and I jumped up and down like a couple of kids. The players were piling all over each other on the field, tossing their Warrior pads and sticks in the air. It was pandemonium—and it was beautiful.

I remember looking for Dave on the field, and not being able to find him. That's because, right after the game ended, he tossed all his gear and his jersey in a pile on the field and ran into the stands. He just stood there and watched his teammates and coaches celebrate on the field. The game had been so stressful, so emotional for him, all he wanted to do was take a step back and watch everyone else whoop it up. Standing there, realizing his company was enjoying its greatest moment, Dave came to a monumental decision.

He decided that he would never play competitive lacrosse again.

And he never did.

○

Tim, Dave, and I had a meeting scheduled for seven the next morning. I'm an early riser, so a 7 A.M. meeting was no big deal for me. But Dave had just won the world championships. Not surprisingly, after the game he and his teammates went out partying—and didn't stop partying until 5 A.M.

Now, Dave hadn't met Tim yet, so this would be Tim's first impression of the guy I touted as the heart and soul of our new enterprise. Dave walked in—to his credit, right on time—with his head completely shaved (he shaved it himself the night before the game because he thought it made him look tougher). He was clearly drained and exhausted.

And the only reason he wasn't hungover was because he was still drunk.

The three of us had breakfast in a little local coffee shop, and we talked about the incredible championship game. Dave was sharp as a tack—he told us how he personally knew all the players, and how many of them were under contract with Warrior. He explained how he had told them about our idea for a league, and how they were all gung ho to get involved. Dave's passion for the sport poured out of him. And Tim Robertson, still on a high from watching the championship game, just sat there soaking it all up. There was so much energy at that table you could have lit up half of Baltimore.

That's when Tim said, "I'm in."

So that little breakfast, as much as any other event, marks the true beginning of Major League Lacrosse.

The irony, of course, is that the disaster of the U.S. team surrendering its ten-goal lead turned out to be a really lucky break for us. It created all this excitement that got us even more fired up about starting a pro league. Had the U.S. won in a rout, we wouldn't have felt a fraction of the euphoria we experienced watching the double-OT win.

The excitement of that victory lit the fuse at the end of our rocket. All we could think was, *Look out, lacrosse world, here we come!*

○

Tim and I wound up kicking in a nice chunk of change to get the league off the ground. Then I turned to Dave. Now, I knew he didn't have a whole lot of money, but I felt it was important that he ante up whatever he could for the league. I felt that investing our own money would bond us as partners, as a team.

"So, Dave," I asked him, "how much money can you put into this deal?"

"None, Jake, but thanks for asking."

He was kidding, but not really. At the time he was scraping out a living through Warrior. The only money he had was $70,000 he had recently inherited from his grandfather's estate. I didn't know that at the time—I didn't really know what his finances were at all. If I had known that all he had in the world was his grandfather's dough, I don't think I would have pushed him as hard as I did to invest. But I reasoned that he had to kick in something, to legitimize his role in launching MLL. So I pushed him.

Dave, once again to his credit, kicked in his whole inheritance.

It wasn't easy for him. That was his life savings—every penny he had. His parents had wanted him to use it to buy a house and start a new life with his wife. Instead Dave invested in his new life with *me*.

When he told his mother what he'd done, she was distraught. I think Dave was pretty much in shock himself. I'm sure he figured I would be the money guy and he would be the lacrosse guy. But I felt that at the start we all needed to contribute equally.

So the kid put in everything he had.

Now we had our core partnership in place: the fitness guru, the Ivy League kid, and the media mogul. To some, we may have seemed like an oddball trio. To me, we were an unbeatable team.

But here's an important rule of succeeding in business: know what you know, and know what you *don't* know.

The truth is that, while Tim, Dave, and I each brought our own unique set of skills to the table, none of us had any experience in the world of pro sports leagues.

I had to find someone who knew his way around the sports world. I had to bring in a man who worked at the highest level of pro sports. So I went to the guy who helped turn the National Football League into one of America's most profitable enterprises.

I had to bring in Frankie V.

You know how in Major League Baseball they have the seventh-inning stretch? Everybody stands up, moves around, gets the blood going after seven innings of wolfing down hot dogs? Well, back in 1994 I had a thought: *How come there's nothing like that in the NFL?*

And because I'm not the type to put an idea on a to-do list and get to it later, I called the vice president of NFL Properties, Frank Vuono, and asked him the same thing. What if I were to go on the field between the third and fourth quarters and lead a stadium full of crazed football fans in a fun, fast, 90-second stretching drill, and at the end of the bit have 100,000 people raise their arms and yell, "Touchdown!"? How about we give that a try?

Frank said, "I love it! Let's do it."

So there I was on the field at Arrowhead Stadium in Kansas City on a crisp fall day in 1994, a few hours before the Kansas City Chiefs would play the Los Angeles Rams. I was rehearsing my "3rd Quarter Fitness Break by Jake" with the Chiefs cheerleaders, and it was going great—lots of energy, lots of fun. At the end of my bit, I had the cheerleaders raise their arms and yell, "Touchdown!" Even the ground crew got in on the action. I finished rehearsal confident that this was going to be a big hit.

Afterward I went up to meet the Chiefs' owner, Lamar Hunt, and hang out with some NFL Properties execs. Now listen, I'm the most optimistic guy in the world. But for some reason I turned to one of the execs and said, "The only thing that can mess this up is if the Chiefs are losing or if it rains."

The guy said, "Don't worry, the Chiefs have Joe Montana"—only the best quarterback in the world—"and the Rams are 0 and 3. And by the way, the forecast says it's going to be gorgeous. So don't sweat it, Jake, you're going to be a hit."

Next thing you know, I'm standing in the tunnel that leads out to the field, waiting to go on with 17 seconds left in the third quarter.

The Chiefs are losing 17–0.

And it's pouring.

The NFL exec said to me, "Look, Jake, I know they've been promoting you on the JumboTron the whole game, but you don't have to go out there if you don't want to." He must have felt like a Roman centurion about to uncage the lions.

I said, "Yes, I do." So I did.

I ran onto the field and got all these drenched and gloomy Chiefs fans out of their seats and on their feet. I launched into my routine, and I could see a stadium full of people in rain slickers and soggy caps just jumping up and down and having a blast. And at the end of it, the whole crowd raised their arms and yelled out, "Touchdown!"— something they hadn't been able to do all game.

What a great moment. Even though the NFL fitness break never caught on, it sure was a lot of fun for everybody that day. Hey, you gotta take a shot, right?

I remember another great NFL moment, when Frank Vuono invited me to a pre–Super Bowl event right around that time. He was going to introduce me to a crowd of retailers and executives, and I would give one of my motivational speeches.

Now, Frank is this big Jersey guy who looks like Tony Soprano in a suit. And seeing as I like to have a little fun onstage, especially with a CEO or president of a company, when Frank introduced me I convinced him to get down and give me 50 push-ups. I told him if he did it, the Super Bowl would get monster ratings that year (that was my way of pumping him up, and getting the crowd pumped up as well). So Frank got down in his nice suit and banged out 50 push-ups. The crowd got a big kick out it, and Frank was a good sport, too.

Frank Vuono, by the way, was one of the most influential marketing executives in sports at the time—a guy who revolutionized the way NFL football is watched and enjoyed in this country. He basically turned NFL players from anonymous athletes hidden beneath helmets into superstars. He took the licensing of NFL-related products from a $300 million business to a $2.5 *billion* business. I knew him as a guy who was open to new ideas and had the guts to try something exciting.

And that's exactly why I called him.

The big question was, would I be able to persuade a former NFL bigwig to get involved with launching our league?

Hey, I got him to do push-ups in a suit in front of a thousand people, didn't I? So, I liked my chances.

○

Frank grew up in Lyndhurst, New Jersey, and spent his childhood chasing his two older brothers around. Playing sports with the older kids made him tough and fearless, and he might have had a shot at playing tight end in the NFL if he hadn't torn his medial collateral ligament (MCL) his senior year at Princeton. Instead, he went to work in advertising, and then for the NFL.

Frank also had a connection to lacrosse, which came in handy for me. When he was at Princeton, he walked by a field and saw a bunch of guys running around doing something he didn't recognize. He was mesmerized by the action—it seemed like the perfect combination of football and hockey, two of his favorite sports. So he pulled one student aside and asked what he was playing.

"Lacrosse," the student told him.

"Man, I have to play this game," Frank said.

Frank didn't make the team at Princeton, but he became a big fan of the sport. In fact, when I called him in 1998 and asked him if he was interested in helping us launch a pro outdoor lacrosse league, he asked if I was by a fax machine.

"I need to send you an interview I gave to *The New York Times* a few years ago," he explained.

In that interview, the reporter asked Frank which small American sport he believed was most ready to explode in popularity. His answer was there in black-and-white: "Lacrosse."

I knew Frankie V. and I were on the same page. And I knew he was a guy who couldn't resist a challenge. So I asked him point-blank, "Help us launch our league."

His response was music to my ears: "I'm in."

Getting Frank on board was a big moment for our team. He knew a lot more about the business of sports than Tim, Dave, or I did. After leaving the NFL, Frank co-founded a sports marketing company, Integrated Sports International (ISI), and he gave us office space in his corporate headquarters in Secaucus, New Jersey. We were able to handle all of the league's early administrative work from there.

Frank was also bringing an NFL mentality to our team. He was going to help us with all the moving parts—developing the logo, naming the teams, picking uniforms, stadium contracts, sponsors, you name it. Frank loved having the opportunity to put everything he'd ever learned throughout his legendary career into practice. He loved the opportunity to be in on the ground floor of a professional sports league.

Plus, he knew from experience that little baby sports leagues can grow up to become big giant sports leagues. He cited the example of the American Football League (AFL), an upstart football league created in 1960 by some owners who couldn't buy teams in the NFL. The league launched with eight teams, and early attendance numbers weren't great. Few people gave the AFL much chance to succeed.

But eventually the AFL had grown so popular—thanks to star athletes like Joe Namath—that it merged with the NFL. Frank knew how in time an upstart league could become the real deal, and he wanted to help us make that happen with our league.

Listen, we both knew we weren't going to be the NFL overnight. Frank was also worried that we might be slightly ahead of the curve:

that the tipping point for lacrosse—the moment when it would become a popular, mainstream sport in the U.S.—was potentially a while away.

But he knew he was seeing more and more kids walking around with lacrosse sticks in his neighborhood. He knew lacrosse had some of the most passionate, loyal fans he'd ever met. He believed lacrosse had every chance of becoming a top American sport one day. So he was willing to take a chance and hop on board, and we were thrilled to have him.

I wanted Dave to meet Frank, so I set up a meeting. Here's how Dave remembers it:

> I knew that Frank Vuono was a pioneer in the sports marketing business and someone who was really respected in the sports world, so I was pretty happy that Jake was able to recruit him for our league. He was this big, boisterous, larger-than-life guy—a real straight shooter—and I remember thinking it was pretty cool to be meeting him.
>
> So what did Jake do? By way of introducing me to Frank, he said, "Dave is the founder of a $27 million company."
>
> "That's very impressive, Dave," Frank said, while I tried to keep a straight face.
>
> Jake had only overstated the worth of my company by roughly $26 million.
>
> The meeting went well, and later I pulled my partner aside. "Why in the world did you tell Frank that Warrior is worth $27 million?" I asked. "We'll be lucky to clear $1 million in sales this year."
>
> "Listen, kid," Jake said, "I have faith that someday Warrior will be worth $27 million. Now let me ask you: do *you* believe it'll be worth that someday?"
>
> I thought about it, and said, "Yeah, I do."
>
> "Then what I told Frank is true."

For Jake, it was that simple. And then he shared one of his key philosophies with me, something I will never forget.

He said, "The world lets you be what you make it believe you are."

If you believe in your dreams, he said, other people will believe in them, too. The vision that you have for yourself *becomes* the reality. Now, I was still caught up in the nickel-and-dime worries of launching my little equipment company. To be honest, I'd never really stopped long enough to think of Warrior as a multimillion-dollar business. Jake's lesson to me was that unless I *dreamed* big, I would never *be* big.

Look, I'll never be as in-your-face and out there as Jake. I'll never be his equal when it comes to sheer chutzpah. But although I'd only been around him for a few weeks, he was already starting to change the way I thought. He was starting to change the way I saw the world.

Jake was opening my eyes to a much bigger game.

I really liked the team we had in place so far: me, Dave, Tim, and Frank. But I knew we had to keep adding pieces to the puzzle. And the logical next step was to bring in a big-time sponsor.

Early on in the game, the only sponsor we had was Dave's company, Warrior. But one thing Warrior couldn't provide us with was shoes. And that gave us the opportunity to go after a major shoe sponsor. And you know me—if I'm going to reach out to someone, I'm going to reach out to the top guy. So I called the man who put Reebok on the map.

I called my buddy Angel Martinez.

I knew Angel from back in my fitness-training days. He signed me to a deal with Reebok in the mid-80s, around the time he was launching a new fitness shoe. Angel is a remarkable guy. His parents brought him to the U.S. from Cuba when he was three, and as a youngster he became a serious long-distance runner. He chose running because he wasn't the biggest guy in the world, and never got picked when kids chose up teams for baseball. Running wasn't something you had to be tall and muscular to do well. "The clock never lies," Angel would say. "The clock doesn't care." He became a pretty accomplished amateur runner, and after college opened a running-shoe store, Starting Line Sports, in the Bay Area. His thinking was simple: *Let me try to make a living out of my passion for running.*

He pulled it off—and then some.

The store did really well, and Angel was recruited to join a brand-new shoe company. In this way, he became the third employee ever hired by Reebok.

In his time there, Angel created the first aerobic shoe, and pioneered a lot of marketing techniques that helped the company become a giant in the industry. He started at Reebok as a sales rep and would eventually leave as Chief Marketing Officer.

I also knew that Angel's son played lacrosse, and that Angel had fallen in love with the game watching him play. So by the time I called him with my pitch, I knew he'd already been bitten by the lacrosse bug. I told him how we planned to start the league, and I asked if he was interested in having Reebok sign on as a sponsor and develop a new lacrosse shoe.

Angel immediately saw an opportunity for Reebok. He liked that lacrosse was an authentic American sport, and he believed that once people got exposed to it, they tended to fall in love with it . . . just like we all had.

Mainly, he loved lacrosse for what it represented: it gave anyone of any size the chance to compete. There's a spot on the field for kids of every size, and many great athletes who aren't big enough to play football or basketball end up playing lacrosse. Lacrosse gives a lot of people what running gave Angel: an opportunity to shine.

"If lacrosse had been an option for me as a kid," Angel told me, "I never would have run."

I didn't have to sell Angel on lacrosse. He was already a believer.

"So," I asked him, "are you in?"

"Yes."

Boom! We now had a major sponsor.

Even so, Angel had some reservations. He wanted to be sure Reebok get plenty of exposure as a sponsor of our league, but at that point we didn't have a TV deal in place—in fact, we barely had an office with a TV *set*. So while Angel loved the idea of the league and agreed to come on board, he wanted to see how things shook out before giving us a long-term commitment.

Even so, I felt we now had enough going for us to make everything official. Time to let the world know that our league was on its way.

○

In our new Secaucus offices, we started making our dream come alive. For one thing, we settled on an official name for the league. We tossed around a couple of different names, but from the start we all referred to our baby as Major League Lacrosse, and that's what stuck. We knew we wanted it to have a three-letter acronym, just like the big boys—the NBA, the NFL, the NHL, MLB. So, that's what we became—MLL.

Then we had to come up with a logo. At Warrior, Dave used a couple of young brothers from Colorado who had their own company, Vivid Designs, so we decided to go with them. Dave had already begun fooling around with an image—a helmeted lacrosse player holding a stick and running. Our Colorado brothers used a photo of one of our players, Michael Watson, to create a silhouette, which they believed symbolized "every player" and communicated at a glance the nature of our organization. They drew sharp lines behind the silhouette to suggest motion, excitement, and "edginess." They put the silhouette inside a shield shape meant to look like the net on top of a lacrosse stick. That shape was not only a natural for us but was also entirely unique among pro sports logos, making ours instantly recognizable. And above the silhouette they put three big letters: MLL.

Our logo, if I say so myself, was awesome.

Next, we needed a slogan. The main thing we needed our slogan to do was separate us from an indoor box lacrosse league that was in operation at the time. Indoor lacrosse is played in arenas on hockey rinks without the ice. It is to outdoor lacrosse what arena football is to the NFL.

We were going to play lacrosse the way it was meant to be played: outdoors, on a big field, with plenty of space for great players to do their thing. So our slogan had to reflect what was new and special about us.

We also wanted the slogan to be a little in-your-face—just like the league would be. Remember when you were in school, and you had a problem with a kid and would say, "Come on, let's take it outside"? It's what you say when you want to mix it up and settle a score. Well, that was the first thing that popped into our minds when we were thinking about a slogan. Plus, the double meaning really worked for us —we were literally taking lacrosse outdoors.

So that became our slogan: "Take It Outside."

Now we were really ready to go public. And what better place to do so than Times Square in New York City?

We booked the All-Star Café, a big, splashy, sports-themed restaurant right in the heart of Times Square, and we scheduled our inaugural press conference for May 24, 1999. *Look out world, here we come!*

Then, four days before the announcement, my wife, Tracey, had our third child, Zach, joining big sister Morgan and brother Nick.

Let's just say we had a *really* busy week.

On May 24, Tim, Angel, and Frank joined Dave and me at the All-Star Café for the press conference. This was going to be our big moment in the sun. Dave rounded up a handful of top lacrosse players, and we also arranged for some younger players to be there, to highlight our sport's appeal among America's youth. We had huge amounts of food, and Dave supplied Warrior merchandise we could hand out to reporters and fans. He really went all out for the press conference, bringing in a small fortune in logoed T-shirts, bags, hats, and sticks—a beautiful mountain of swag.

We had a big blowup of our logo that we would dramatically unveil. We had giant posters emblazoned with Take It Outside. We had microphones set up all over the place and 100 seats to accommodate all the media. We made room for all the cameras that would capture the action.

Everyone was nervous but super excited. We had all prepared something to say, and I stressed to everyone to stay on message. "This is New York City, fellas," I said, "and these New York City press people are really tough."

Finally, we threw open the doors.

And all of three people walked in.

That's right, three members of the media bothered to come. One was from a lacrosse magazine we'd never heard of. Another was from a local Jewish newspaper. The third guy just sat there eating a jelly donut. I don't even know where he was from.

There were four times as many people on the dais as there were in the seats.

Well, you know me—I always look for the silver lining. So I turned to Dave and said, "Hey, at least we don't have to give away all those T-shirts."

At the end of the day, there were still three people there who came to hear our announcement, so we went ahead and put on a show. I told our guys, "Try to imagine that the place is packed." We unveiled our new logo, touted our new slogan, showed off our star players, and announced that Major League Lacrosse would launch in the summer of 2000. Right then and there, we all realized there was no turning back.

The whole world now knew MLL was in business . . . okay, at least those three people did.

And you know, to this day I have no idea where that jelly-donut guy was from.

Just four days after our earth-shattering press conference, we got a chance to promote our new league at the single biggest lacrosse event at the time: the NCAA Final Four.

Sure, the World Championships were a big deal, but they came around only once every four years. The annual Final Four was lacrosse's college Super Bowl, and in the late 1990s it started drawing tens of thousands of crazed lacrosse fans. The 1999 Final Four would be held at Byrd Stadium on the campus of the University of Maryland in College Park, and as many as 30,000 people were expected for the weekend. We knew this was an opportunity we couldn't pass up.

So that weekend, we set up in the parking lot of Byrd Stadium, right where all the fans would be streaming in. We sectioned off an area, set up a tent, and brought in two cars with MLL logos all over them. Angel was there, and so were some of our star players, ready to meet the fans and sign autographs. And swag? We had some *serious* swag—posters, hats, sticks, T-shirts, the works. This wasn't going to be like the press conference, where we couldn't give our stuff away. This was going to be a can't-miss, home-run promotional bonanza.

There was only one problem.

We weren't allowed to be there.

You see, the NCAA is the leading amateur athletic association in the country, and they can't associate with any professional sports enterprise. In other words, they couldn't have anything to do with Reebok, Warrior, or MLL.

But, you know, the chance to promote our league to the most rabid lacrosse fans in the country was just too tempting an opportunity for us to pass up. So we set up shop in the parking lot anyway, guerilla-style.

This was Occupy Byrd Stadium.

And let me tell you, the response we got from fans was *overwhelming*. The people were fired up about the prospect of a pro outdoor league. Pretty much everyone told us the same thing: "This is exactly what this sport needs." Sure, a few people were skeptical, asking questions like, "How are you going to get this funded?" (Hey pal, let us worry about that.) But the vast majority of fans were thrilled by the idea of having their own lacrosse team to cheer for.

Our coming-out party was feeling a whole lot better than our press conference . . . until some NCAA officials spotted us and chased us out of the parking lot.

Or at least they thought they did.

We packed up our stuff and scampered away like a bunch of high-school trespassers, but we weren't finished yet. Instead of leaving, we moved our operation behind a car and kept a lookout for the NCAA guys, and we continued talking to fans and handing out sticks and talking up our great new league.

Okay, so maybe that's not how the NFL got started.

But the point is, we didn't get discouraged when they chased us out of the parking lot. We kept going.

That's pretty much the story of Major League Lacrosse. We just kept going.

I guess we didn't know any better.

Of course, we could talk all we wanted about how great our league was going to be, but unless we raised the money, there wasn't going to be a league. It was time for Dave and me to go out and beat the bushes and find some real investors. I would set up the meetings and do most of the pitching, while Dave would work the lacrosse angle and talk about all the great players he knew and the growth of the sport.

For me, it would be a chance to mingle with some of my Hollywood pals.

For Dave, it would be the shock of his life.

○

Since Dave showed up in Hollywood and started hanging out with me, we've had a lot of wacky stuff happen to us (of course, *everyone* in Hollywood has a lot of wacky stuff happen to them). Maybe the weirdest thing that happened to Dave took place just a couple of years ago, when he was attacked by Warren Beatty.

That's right, my partner in Major League Lacrosse was terrorized by an Oscar winner.

We were in the valet parking lot outside L.A.'s Giorgio Baldi restaurant, which overlooks the Pacific Ocean and is in my opinion the best Italian restaurant in the world. There were paparazzi everywhere, and we were getting blinded by flashbulbs. We were squeezed into my new Smart Car—a far cry from a Ferrari, yes indeed. This thing was basically a clown car—it was about the size of a closet, with red wheels and a neat racing stripe I put on it for my kids. I'm sure Dave and I looked pretty funny inside it, but I loved driving it around town.

Anyway, a big black limo pulled into the lot, and out stepped my old pal Warren Beatty. Warren had always known me as a guy who likes a fancy set of wheels, so when he spotted me in the Smart Car, he just couldn't believe it. In fact, he went a little nuts about it.

"Jesus, Jake, a Smart Car?" he screamed in mock outrage. "You have to be kidding me! When did you go green?"

And then he attacked us.

He started messing with the car, getting on it, in it, over it, rocking it from side to side, really giving us a hard time. The paparazzi were snapping away at Warren going ballistic. I was laughing my tail off, because I know he likes to have a little fun.

But Dave? He didn't know *what* was going on. He sat in the passenger seat watching Warren jump on the hood and rock the car, and he was thinking that one of Hollywood's most famous actors was about to turn the car upside down. Dave was in a *panic.*

"Jake, Jake, make him stop!" he pleaded. "Either get him off the car or drive this tin can out of here!"

Hey Dave, welcome to L.A.

Dave was the ultimate fish out of water in Hollywood, but the fact is, I had once been the new kid on the block, too. I was this guy from New York with a thick Long Island accent, and suddenly I'm hanging out with Steven Spielberg and Harrison Ford? I go from shooting the breeze with my pals in Baldwin to flying in private jets and eating caviar with a spoon with Weils?

Or get a load of this story: I was in Weils's bungalow at Amblin Entertainment, his film company on the lot of Universal Studios. We had just finished a workout when he told me that he had to run out for a quick meeting. He said he had a friend coming over to meet him there, and would I mind waiting until he got back? I figured, hey, there's always really good food in Weils's office, so why not?

Then this tall, ultra glamorous woman walked in—big hair, dark sunglasses, fancy dress, the whole bit. She sat down and said nothing. After a while, I felt like I had to break the ice, so I said, "Hey, how you doing?" By the way, I was looking pretty dashing myself, with my tight T-shirt and worn-out gray sweatpants.

Still, she said nothing. Total silence. I kept trying.

There were awards and plaques all over the office, so I said, "Boy, this guy sure has won a lot of awards, hasn't he?"

No luck—not a peep. *Awkward* silence.

Finally, Weils came back and said, "Oh, Jake, I see you've met Sophia Loren."

I was absolutely a fish out of water in those early days in Hollywood, but the truth is I *loved* being in that situation. It was one big, fun adventure for me, and I just went along for the ride, soaking it all up. Through my fitness-motivation business, I got to learn from the most successful people in the world what it takes to be a success, and that was *way* better than any college course I could have taken.

Now it was my turn to take Dave along for the ride.

In our early discussions about the league, we came up with a dollar figure we felt we needed to reach in order to launch MLL. It wasn't a fortune, but it wasn't chump change either. I had made a lot of friends in Hollywood over the years, and I wasn't shy about approaching them for help. I wasn't exactly going to pass the hat around, but I *was* going to ask my friends to introduce me to people who might be interested in investing in a pro sports league.

One of the first guys I went to was my pal Jeff Berg, chairman and CEO of International Creative Management (ICM), the big Hollywood talent agency. He was one of my original Body by Jake clients, and he steered me toward someone he knew who'd had a lot of success in the sports and movie businesses.

"He has some great ideas for marketing your league," Jeff told me, "and he'd like to discuss them with you."

Terrific—Dave and I were all ears. If Jeff was speaking so highly of him, I told Dave, he had to be the real deal. So we were pretty excited when we showed up in this guy's Los Angeles office for our meeting.

Very quickly, though, it became apparent he had some really wild ideas about our league. He'd been the producer of some popular action films, and he envisioned MLL as just another big-budget action movie—*Clash of the Titans* with goalies. He whipped out an elaborate storyboard depicting his Cecil B. DeMille vision for the league. I'm talking a field that looked like a battleground from *Apocalypse Now*, with water hazards, sandpits, scaling walls, and even shooting flames and incendiary bombs like you see in rock concerts!

I'm not kidding!

"You're not planning on blowing any of our guys to pieces, are you?" I asked half-jokingly.

"Don't worry, no one's gonna get really hurt," said the producer, whom we'll call Gladiator Guy.

Now while I'm sitting there listening to this crazy pitch about how to turn MLL into *Rollerball* meets *Armageddon III*, Dave is sitting next to me wondering what he's gotten himself into. And the reason I know he's freaking out is because he's got the jittery legs going.

When Dave gets really excited, his legs start twitching and pumping like there's no tomorrow. And on that day, those legs were bouncing up and down to the point that when I looked down, I realized that *my* legs were bouncing! My legs never bounce! But Dave was so freaking jittery that he got me doing it, too! I willed my legs to calm down, but Dave was hopeless. His legs had a mind of their own, and that mind was getting blown right now.

Then Gladiator Guy brought in someone he introduced as his "marketing genius." Apparently this guy had done promotion for some foreign sports teams. He was full of ideas as well, and he told us about his most successful promotion, for a Russian hockey team.

The promotion? Toilet Paper Day.

That's right, I can't make this stuff up. This guy gave away rolls and rolls of toilet paper because "the Russians have a hard time getting toilet paper," he explained. "Thousands of people turned out. *Thousands!*"

Dave's legs were pumping so fast he could have powered an energy grid.

I wanted to say thanks and get the heck out of there, but Dave's legs were so wobbly I didn't think he could stand up. Eventually, we said our good-byes and got out of Dodge.

"These are your marketing geniuses, Jake?" Dave barked. "Land mines and toilet paper? *Are you kidding me?*"

To this day Dave believes that the meeting was an elaborate practical joke.

I told him we had to shrug it off and move on. Hollywood's a weird place, and we were going to meet our share of chuckleheads. But there was a bright side, I told him.

"What's that?"

"At least we know things can't get any weirder than that."

Boy, was I wrong.

○

Not long after our disaster with Gladiator Guy, Dave and I were in New York City to meet with another potential investor. This guy was like no one else you have ever met. We'll call him the Mad Man.

"He is a brilliant advertising guy, one of the most creative people in the universe," I told Dave.

At least I got that right—this guy was not from our galaxy.

Dave and I met at Da Silvano's restaurant, one of the finest Italian restaurants in Manhattan. Hey, if there's one thing Dave and I always did, it was eat great food. Italian, sushi, steaks, you name it. You've got to understand—we took a lot of investor meetings, and we struck out a lot. So we figured, if we're going to get rejected when we're asking for dough, we might as well at least enjoy a great meal.

So there we were at Da Silvano's, waiting for the Mad Man.

And waiting . . . and waiting . . . for more than an hour.

Dave's legs were already on warp speed.

Now, I knew about the Mad Man, and I knew he was a little—how do I put it?—different. Some big magazine had just called him "a crazy genius brand guru," and both those words applied—genius *and* crazy. I told Dave that the Mad Man was known for boosting sales and profits in industries ranging from fashion to fast food. When it came to the business of branding, he was the real deal.

"But you gotta prepare yourself for this guy," I warned. "He's a little showy. So just be ready, okay, buddy?"

When he finally arrived, Dave was *not* ready.

First two huge security guys walked into Da Silvano's. One of them talked into his collar, like a Secret Service agent, and said, "The Big Man is in the house." Then, the Mad Man sauntered in. He was 400 pounds of human piled on top of two stumpy legs. He was only about five foot eight, but when he walked it seemed like he sent shock waves through the place. He was wearing Phat Farm jeans, round tortoiseshell glasses, and a humongous yellow rain slicker. I swear, the guy looked like the Penguin from *Batman.* Behind him were a couple more flunkies and a very young, very shapely woman—his wife. Like the Penguin was married to Jessica Rabbit.

The restaurant suddenly came alive. Waiters were flushed out of every corner and swooped in bearing huge trays laden with Italian appetizers. The Mad Man plopped down at our table and devoured the food as quickly as it showed up, shoveling it into his mouth right

JAKE STEINFELD and DAVE MORROW

off the plates while he talked. He ate so fast that as much food flew out of his mouth as made it down his gullet.

I felt the table shaking violently. Dave's legs.

"Hey Jake, who is dis guy wit you?" the Mad Man asked. "You say he went to Princeton? No freakin' way this guy went to Princeton." Then he turned to Dave. "What dorm you live in? I went to Princeton, and I didn't see you there."

Dave was too shell-shocked to answer.

"Hey, I'm talking to you! What are you, deaf and dumb?"

Before Dave could respond, the Mad Man yelled for "the dumb bastard water boy" and ordered him to "get your ass over here and get me some more freakin' bread!" Except he didn't say "freakin'." Let's keep this book family friendly.

Then we noticed that while the Mad Man was ranting and raving and stuffing food in his mouth, he was also motioning to his driver, a guy in a three-piece Armani suit standing at attention next to our table. The Mad Man was making flicking motions with his fingers, like some kind of weird code. And in response, the driver was repeatedly flicking himself in the head.

Huh?

"Joey!" the Mad Man screamed at his driver. "Come here, I want to eat your freakin' head!"

The Mad Man put a small plate of olive oil on the edge of our table. Then he pointed at the plate. Joey, without a word, bent down and dipped his forehead in the olive oil, and held it there.

The Mad Man grabbed a big steak knife and pretended to cut Joey's neck while laughing like a maniac. Finally, Joey straightened up, stepped back, and stood at attention again. Olive oil ran down his face and all over his Armani suit.

Huh?

Now *everyone* in the restaurant was staring at us in horror.

And Dave's legs were going like a *piston*.

"Jake, what the hell is going on?" he whispered to me. "Why would that guy let his boss do that to him?"

"He must get paid a whole lot of money," I answered.

The Mad Man was just getting started. Suddenly, he was screaming like Joe Pesci in *Goodfellas*: *"I want plates of meat and fish! The big plates! Bring 'em out, you know what I want! The big plates, the BIG PLATES!"*

A conga line of waiters came out of the kitchen with enormous plates piled high with steak, tuna, and pasta. The Mad Man grabbed two huge forks, one in each hand, and stabbed the big mounds of food like they were still alive. He stuffed big forkfuls into his mouth one after the other until his cheeks were completely puffed out. Whole entrées spewed from his mouth. I mean, the guy looked like his heart was about to explode. We were having dinner with Jabba the Hutt.

And in the middle of it all, he turned to Dave and asked, "So, do you have kids?"

Like they were just two guys shooting the breeze.

"Uh, no, I just got married and we don't have kids yet," Dave said.

"Freakin' kids make me crazy!" the Mad Man screamed, spewing more food at Dave.

"Oh, don't be silly," his young wife said.

Then the Mad Man's beeper went off and he threw it against the wall, shattering it into a million pieces.

Dave's legs were flying around like he was a Rockette.

In fact, let me have him tell you how the rest of our meeting went himself:

> I just remember this guy screaming at me and wondering why I wasn't answering him.
>
> "Jake, what the hell is wrong with your buddy here? Does this Detroit yahoo ever open his yap? Why is he staring at me? Is he hot for me?"
>
> I was staring at him because I really felt like my brain was going to melt.
>
> Look, when I started out with Jake on MLL, I was living kind of a double life. Back in Detroit I was this mild-mannered, suburban, blue-collar hump, struggling to keep my start-up business afloat. I spent my days in the metal shop, packing boxes, or meeting with suppliers and

bankers. There was absolutely nothing glamorous about my existence.

Then Jake would swoop in and summon me to L.A. or the Hamptons or Manhattan, and the roller coaster would start up again.

I'd try to find a cheap flight, usually with no success, and off I'd go to an alternate universe, where guys wear $50,000 watches and drive different-colored Ferraris every day of the week. I'd be sitting with Jake's friends while they yammered on about their vacation in St. Barts and at the same time be nervous as hell that the hotel clerk was going to reject my credit card.

So when I met the Mad Man, I had to ask myself, *Is this really happening or am I dreaming?*

Yet the dinner at Da Silvano's was only the beginning. Jake and I got swept out of the restaurant and into one of the Mad Man's waiting SUVs, which was decked out with black windows, bulletproof body armor, flashing lights, several sirens, and a tricked-out dashboard packed with emergency-band radios from every police and fire department in the city. I also noticed a bunch of bulletproof jackets and a small arsenal of weapons.

I was a long, long way from home.

Apparently the Mad Man had ties to New York City's fire department, which had given him a deputy fire marshal's badge. I'm sure they meant it to be honorary, but the Mad Man certainly did not. He put on the sirens and the flashing lights, and we tore through the streets of Manhattan with him on a loudspeaker ordering cars and taxis and pedestrians to get out of his way. This guy believed he was some kind of crime-fighting superhero cruising the streets of the city on the lookout for bad guys. I silently cursed Jake for getting me into this mess.

We stopped at a police station, where the Mad Man yelled at Jake to put on a fitness demonstration for the cops. But before that could happen, something came over the police radio, and suddenly we were all piled back in the SUV.

"We're responding to a domestic-disturbance call," I was told.

Then I heard over the radio that cops were saying "guns are involved."

Okay, so now I was on my way to a crime scene.

When we got there I was ready to refuse to get out of the SUV, but before I could the Mad Man ordered me to stay put. He took Jake along with him instead; I guess he figured Jake would be handier in case something went down—or at least make a better human shield. I sat in the SUV wondering if I'd ever see my friend again.

Finally—after spending 12 hours with this crazy person and not getting a single dime for Major League Lacrosse—Jake and I made it back to our hotel at 3:30 A.M. That's when he tried to put the whole day into perspective.

"We're learning something, though," he told me.

"Oh yeah? What did we possibly learn today?"

"We learned we just may have to do this on our own, buddy."

Dave figured that since I'd been living in Los Angeles for a while, I was used to meetings like the ones we had with Gladiator Guy and the Mad Man.

"Are you nuts?" I told him. "Those were just as weird for me as they were for you." And that was the truth.

But the craziness didn't end there. We must have taken a hundred meetings, not all of them involving guys soaking their heads in olive oil, but most of them frustrating and fruitless. We weren't discriminating—we'd basically meet with anyone who had a checkbook. Most people tossed us out right after we asked them for a couple of million bucks, but we tried not to get too discouraged. We just kept plugging away.

Early on, we had a meeting with a guy who owned his own big-time private equity company. I knew he had played lacrosse in college, so I figured we had a shot with him. But we didn't even have a business plan yet, so Dave asked me what we were going to show this guy when we met him.

"Hey, we'll just give him the rap-a-doo," I told him. "He'll see how fired up we are."

Dave wasn't crazy about that idea. I guess he didn't have as much confidence in the rap-a-doo as I did. "We need a business plan," he insisted. "We can't go into this meeting with nothing."

So he called one of his former Princeton classmates, Brooke Coburn, who worked for an investment bank on Wall Street. Brooke had written the offering memo for Warrior, and knew his way around a business plan. Dave asked him to draw up a plan for Major League Lacrosse, and Brooke said he'd do it.

There was only one hitch, Dave explained. We needed the business plan *the next morning*.

Brooke started working in the afternoon, stayed up all night, and finally finished the plan around 7 A.M. And the thing looked fantastic —beautiful charts, all the numbers in order, really professional. Now all he had to do was get it out to us in Secaucus, which was about an hour's drive away. We got a car service to courier the plan over, and it got there just in time for our meeting with the investor.

Then we dolled up the office, laid out a big spread of food, and put out our shiny new business plan on the table.

The guy didn't even bother to look at the plan, though. He showed up and said he wanted to hear the "vision" for our new league. "Let's just look at this from 10,000 feet," he said.

What do you mean, 10,000 feet? I thought to myself. *Go take a ride in a helicopter if you want 10,000 feet. We're talking business here.*

It was a very short meeting. The guy never opened our business plan or ate our food. Oh yeah, and he didn't invest, either.

But once again, we looked at the bright side.

"Hey Dave," I said, "at least we don't have to go out for lunch today."

Then I sent his pal Brooke, who'd worked so hard on that business plan, a nice bottle of champagne to thank him.

We set up another meeting with a potential investor who said that he was interested in being part of the league, and maybe even buying one of the teams. Evidently he owned a big plumbing company and had some bucks to throw around. Dave and I flew to New York to meet him. I usually stayed in a nice room at the Regency Hotel, but this time I got an even bigger room, to really impress the investor. I wanted him to think, *Hey, I'm playing with the big boys here.*

The guy showed up, and we started talking sports and business. But pretty quickly I discovered something important about him: he didn't own his own plumbing corporation.

Turns out he was a plumber. A plumber who wanted to pitch me on a fitness product he'd dreamed up while fixing toilets.

The plumber was a nice enough guy, so we hung out for a while. But, needless to say, no deal.

Frank Vuono set up another meeting with a prominent investment banker from Baltimore. Finally, somebody who might be legitimate. This guy had dealings with a company that produced artificial turf, and he knew all about lacrosse. Frank said he was a terrific guy, so we were all excited to meet him and present our idea.

Well, this guy walked into our conference room in Secaucus sweating like Albert Brooks in *Broadcast News*. It was a hot day, sure, but he looked like he'd just had lunch in a sauna. He seemed very nervous and kept picking at his forehead. Then we noticed blood trickling down from his brow. Pretty soon he started grabbing his head and trying to wipe the sweat off, and he was smearing blood all over his face. We were sitting there thinking that he was having a heart attack. Finally, we had to call a time-out and bring him a glass of water and a defibrillator just in case. We never learned what was wrong with him, but our best guess was an overactive thyroid.

In any case, it was kind of hard to concentrate on pitching this guy on our league with him bleeding all over our conference table. And guess what? He didn't invest, either. What, are you surprised?

I have to admit, I was starting to get a little frustrated by the number of people who loved our idea but weren't ready to pull the trigger. We heard a lot of "We'll get back to you," and "Call us after you've been around for a few seasons."

So when I heard a venture capitalist say, "Let me think about it" during our next meeting, I guess I snapped a little.

This guy was actually the CEO of his own venture fund in Washington, D.C., and was a real big shot in the financial world. Dave knew him through his Princeton and Wall Street connections, and described him as the ultimate whale. We pitched the league to him over the phone, and he said he was really interested, so we flew out to see him—me from L.A., and Dave from Detroit. Hey, we logged thousands and thousands of miles flying across the country, because we always believed the next meeting was going to be *the* meeting, and the next guy was going to be *the* guy. I guess that just comes from being positive and passionate . . . and a little insane.

Anyway, we had a fantastic lunch, like we always did, and talked a lot about lacrosse. Everything was going so well that we started feeling like this might be the guy to take us to the promised land. So after lunch, we offered him a ride to the airport for a flight he was catching, hoping we could spend a little more time with him and seal the deal.

Yet every time we brought it up on the ride to the airport, this guy just didn't bite. We were getting closer and closer to the departures terminal, so we stepped up our pleading. But he didn't want to talk business.

Finally, we pulled up to the terminal, and Dave went to open the limo door for the CEO to get out. That's when I reached over and locked it.

"We're not finished yet," I said.

Dave gave me his "What the hell are you doing?!" look. He and I were sitting on one side in the back of the limo, the CEO and his assistant on the other. We stared at each other for a few moments, scoping each other out. It was like the O.K. Corral back there.

"So what's it gonna be?" I finally said. "Are you in or out?"

"Let me think about it," the CEO said.

"Well, that's not the right answer."

The CEO squirmed in his seat. Yes, he was a big dog in his industry, but at that moment he was just one more guy blowing us off. And we were getting tired of getting blown off.

"I need to know *now*," I told him. "Are you in or out?"

Dave looked at me as if to say, "Jake, you're losing your mind. Simmer down."

I stared at the guy. The seconds ticked by. The tension mounted. Who was going to win, him or me?

And then he said, "I told you, I'll think about it."

Dave unlocked the door. What were we going to do, keep him back there forever? The CEO and his assistant got their bags, ran out, and never looked back.

I turned to Dave and said, "So what do you think?"

"I think . . . it's a no."

Okay, so maybe we weren't off to a flying start when it came to raising capital. Clearly, it was going to be harder than we expected. We had to start rethinking our approach to funding the league. Instead of an array of founding investors, maybe we could round up some top-notch entrepreneurs to buy teams and fund the league that way.

But before we could do that, I had to address one of the major concerns that Frank Vuono had: he was concerned about the players.

Frankie V. came from the NFL, and he was used to star players with big paychecks and bigger egos. He knew we'd have to be able to control player salaries to have any chance of sustaining the league past a single season. He believed that unless our players were humble and accessible and willing to go the extra mile to win over fans, it would be extremely hard to make the league work.

So he asked me if I thought our players fit that description. What kind of people, he was basically asking me, were we getting into business with?

The truth is, I didn't really know.

Up until then, I trusted Dave's judgment about the players. He told me they were great guys and that we had nothing to worry about. That reassured me—until I remembered that I had told him the Mad Man was a great guy, too. I knew I had to meet the players myself. I had brought Dave into my world; now it was time for him to bring me into his.

I arranged to meet Dave in Michigan at a Warrior Lacrosse Camp he was hosting that summer. Some of the top players were going to be there, so it was the perfect opportunity for me to find out what these guys were all about.

Little did I know they were just as anxious to get the lowdown on me.

In the weeks before I flew to Michigan to meet the players, Dave reached out to all of the top lacrosse guys and spread the word about our league. He knew many of them from his playing days at Princeton, and many more through his company, Warrior. Like him, they were all crazy about the sport, but aside from the World Championships every four years they had no place to channel that passion after college. Sure, a few of them played in the indoor league, but as far as top-notch competition went, they had nowhere to go. For many of these great young players, their glory days—leading college teams to championships—were already behind them.

So when Dave began telling them about our idea for a pro lacrosse league, they were all ears. The pitch was always the same: he'd ask if they'd heard of the Body by Jake guy, then explain how I'd called him out of the blue and sold him on the idea of a league. And most of them said the same thing.

"That guy?"

Okay, so most of the players only knew me as the infomercial guy or from my Family Channel sitcom, *Big Brother Jake*. Because the lacrosse community is very tight-knit, they also viewed me as an out-sider. They wondered, *Why is this Hollywood exercise guru getting in-volved with our sport?* Dave did his best to convey my sincerity and passion for the game. Still, these guys were skeptical, and I knew I had some work to do to earn their trust and win them over.

A couple of months after our press conference, I flew to meet Dave at his summer lacrosse camp in Orchard Lake Village in Michi-gan. I knew I was about to meet some of the top lacrosse players in the world, but I really didn't know what to expect. I'd hung out with plenty of world-class athletes in my day. I knew they could be their own special breed.

I drove to the site of Dave's camp, which was the 125-acre cam-pus of Saint Mary's Preparatory, an all-boys, Catholic prep school on the shores of Orchard Lake. I figured that Dave and the players were staying at a nearby hotel, but Dave told me to meet him in one of the dorms on campus. I walked into this crummy little dorm room, and there he was with a few of the guys.

I thought I'd walked into *Animal House.*

The guys were lying around on beds and cots in their shorts. They barely reacted when I walked in, beyond saying, "Hey man, it's Body by Jake. Cool." There were dirty T-shirts and towels and jock-straps and pizza boxes and beer cans and all sorts of unmentionables all over the floor. A big electric fan was blowing stale air around. I think I may have stepped on a chimichanga. Immediately, I pulled Dave aside.

"Seriously, these are the best players in the world?" I asked him.

"Hey, you wanted to see Dave's World," he said. "Well, here it is."

I hadn't expected these guys to be driving around in Bentleys, but I didn't expect them to look like the cast of *The Hangover,* either. I swear, Mike Tyson's tiger could've come walking out of the bathroom at any minute. My first glimpse of these not-ready-for-prime-time players was a real eye-opener. I realized that lacrosse wasn't anywhere close to being a glamour sport yet.

But soon enough I realized that while these guys may have lacked a little polish, they were also lacking something that could have sunk our league.

These guys had no egos.

For world-class athletes, they were amazingly unpretentious. No agents, no managers, no publicists, no entourage. Dave had about a dozen players there, and to a man they were all good guys. None of them had ever made any real money from lacrosse. They obviously didn't live high on the hog, and they didn't think twice about staying in a dorm room. They weren't playing lacrosse for the money—they were playing the game because they *loved* it.

So I sat in that room with the players, and I told them my ideas for the league. For us to make this work, I told them, we needed the players to be fully on board. They had to understand we were all in it together, building something special from the ground up. So I wanted to make sure the players bought into our way of thinking. I wanted them to understand what they were getting into.

I wanted them to know what they would be: pioneers.

You see, these long-haired guys surrounded by empty beer cans were going to be the Babe Ruths and Michael Jordans of professional outdoor lacrosse. Young kids would put their posters up on their walls. High schoolers would see them in action and be inspired to play pro lacrosse someday. Future sports historians would write about them in hallowed terms. Put simply, these guys were going to be the first true pro lacrosse players the sport had ever known.

They were going to be heroes.

But that didn't mean they were going to get rich.

We planned to pay our players a pretty decent salary. But as with any new pro sports league, our salaries would start at the lower end of the scale. Back in the earlier days of MLB and the NFL, plenty of athletes who'd go on to be Hall of Famers had to take second jobs just to make ends meet. In the 1950s, for instance, New York Yankees Yogi Berra and Whitey Ford sold men's clothes in department stores during the off-season—and Major League Baseball had already been around for decades by then. As late as 1972, Oakland A's relief pitcher Rollie Fingers went back to his job in the stockroom at Sears a few days after the A's won the World Series.

In the NFL, Philadelphia Eagles star Chuck Bednarik, the first pick in the 1949 draft, was nicknamed "Concrete Charlie"—not because he was a ferocious tackler, which he was, but because he sold concrete in the off-season. Even the player considered to be the greatest quarterback of all time, Johnny Unitas, worked in construction to support his family during his early years.

So the players needed to understand that no one involved with Major League Lacrosse would make a lot of money, because there wasn't a lot of money to be made. I told them that all of us had to have the same goal: to make professional outdoor lacrosse a reality, and to make it last. The only way that could happen was for the players to be the very first ambassadors of the game. They would have to meet all the fans, be gracious to every kid, sign every autograph, give every interview, and play every game with unbelievable passion.

Because passion, I told them, always comes first, and everything else follows. When you're passionate about something, great things happen—maybe not overnight, but they do happen. And they happen in a bigger, better way than you could have imagined. So that's what we needed from our players: we needed them to play not for money, but for passion. We needed them to play because they loved the game.

If they did all that, they would be remembered forever as the guys who started it all.

They would be legends.

The truth is, I didn't have to do all that much to convince these guys to play in our league. They were *dying* to play pro lacrosse. They ate, slept, and breathed lacrosse, and for them to get paid a salary to be part of a professional league—well, that was almost too good to be true. All I really had to do was convince them that we were serious, and that we could pull it off.

Here is Dave's description of my first meeting with the players:

> It's true that it was a little like *Animal House* in that dorm. I mean, the players are used to crashing in someone's house and sleeping any old place. That's one of the things we all love about lacrosse: that it's a community of guys who can just get together and play and laugh and hang out.

It's also true that everyone's first reaction to Jake was skepticism. He was this larger-than-life figure, the TV infomercial guy. As I always told the players, "No, Jake is nothing like that. You'll see." And sure enough, when he met them, it didn't take long for them to see he was the real deal. You could tell how passionate he was about lacrosse, how enthusiastic he was about the league. For my guys, it wasn't about selling them on the idea of a league, it was convincing them it was actually going to happen. And Jake did that right away. The players realized he was a regular guy, like them. And that commonality overcame any awkwardness.

After Jake gave them his speech, we took a golf cart and drove over to a field where some other top players were helping out with the kids. Jake introduced himself to everyone, including all these young kids from middle schools and high schools in the area. Then Jake pulled all the kids together, sat them down, and gave them a motivational speech. And, man, no one gives a motivational speech like Jake. He is just so positive, so full of energy, you can't help but get swept up in what he's saying. And the players, they were standing there listening to this speech, too. And they could see how engaged Jake was, how serious he was, and that really convinced them that this was going to happen.

I mean, they knew Jake was this hugely successful guy, and here he was putting his time and his money and his heart into starting this pro lacrosse league, so any hesitation they may have had just disappeared. They were like, "He's serious, he's all over this, let's do it." And that was that. Jake just won them all over, and we now had the best players in the world on board.

Meeting the players was a terrific experience, and I left believing they were committed to being a part of our league.

But their commitment to *practicing?* That, I wasn't so sure about.

Basically, most of these guys were only a few years out of college. And clearly they still liked to party. So I had to wonder: Would they take the league seriously? Would they understand that it was a business, and had to be run like a business? Would we be able to count on them to stay focused?

The answer, as I would soon learn, was—not always.

For the moment, though, I felt pretty good about the makeup of our players. From what I could tell, these were solid, decent guys with a burning desire to play lacrosse. And, bottom line, that's who we were looking for. We wanted to build a league around the best of the best.

One of the decisions we made early on was that the league would not be about any one or two star players. We wanted the face of the league to be the face of *all* of the players. Yes, we were selling our stars—after all, they were the best in the world—but more than that we were selling a great game. We were selling *lacrosse*.

Even so, a couple of players did stand out and become fan favorites. At the time, most people considered Paul and Gary Gait, twin brothers from Canada, to be the two best lacrosse players in the world. They were both three-time All-Americans at Syracuse University, and led the school to three national championships. But the Gait brothers, who in 1999 were 32 years old, weren't affiliated with Dave and Warrior, and for that reason they weren't the guys we put front and center in our league.

Instead, the focus was on a couple of younger players who were considered by many to be two of the best in the game: Mark Millon and Casey Powell. Let me have Dave, who's good friends with both of them, tell you about these guys:

I knew Mark and Casey from playing against them and hanging out with them after games and tournaments. Eventually I hired them to work with me at Warrior. They are both great guys and, like me, they live for lacrosse.

Mark grew up in Long Island and started playing lacrosse in high school after his dad brought home a couple of sticks for him and his brother. But the sticks their dad gave them were the longer sticks used by defensemen, and that was a problem, since Mark knew most of the kids in his neighborhood were playing with shorter sticks used by scorers. So Mark and his brother went into the garage and, just five minutes after getting their sticks, hacksawed them to make them shorter.

"What are you guys doing?" their incredulous dad asked.

"We want to be attackers," Mark said.

And that's what they became. They practiced constantly in their backyard and broke 20 windows in their family's sunroom. They had to do a bunch of chores to pay for new windows, but they never stopped practicing. Once Mark realized he could throw a lacrosse ball at around 90 mph—and once he figured out how much fun that was— he never looked back. He was a three-time All-American at the University of Massachusetts, and then he realized the dream he'd had since he was 12: to play on the U.S. national lacrosse team.

After that, he played a little in the indoor league and went to work for me at Warrior so he could stay close to the game. Mark and I would go out on a sales call, close a deal, then hit the local pub to celebrate. Since we made a lot of sales, we did a lot of celebrating. Nothing wrong with having a little fun while you're trying to succeed in business.

When Mark heard about Jake's idea for a pro league, he knew right away it was a once-in-a-lifetime opportunity for him. He'd never dreamed about playing in a pro league, because there had never been one. Now that MLL was on the horizon, he wanted as much as anyone to make it happen. And he knew we only had one shot at making it work—that if the league failed, no one would dare to try again for a long, long time.

So from the beginning, Mark was all business when it came to the league. He committed to doing whatever it took to make it a reality. I mean, the guy showed up at MLL meetings carrying a briefcase. He was this handsome, clean-cut, all-American guy, and we knew he would be a big asset for the league. That's why Jake and I decided to put him on our original "Take It Outside" poster.

Another player we put on that poster was Casey Powell.

Casey is a fascinating guy. He and his two brothers, Ryan and Mikey, grew up in West Carthage, a tiny town 80 miles north of Syracuse, in upstate New York. Casey's dad worked in a paper mill and his mom was a church secretary, and the family never had much money. But the boys had lacrosse, and that was really all they needed. They knew about the Gait brothers, who were stars at Syracuse at the time, and Casey's single goal in life was to play lacrosse at Syracuse, like his idols. Both he and Ryan got scholarships to the school, and Casey went on to lead the team to a national championship—and be named an All-American four times. He was just one of those brilliant, instinctive, naturally gifted players, and his go-for-broke style made him a huge fan favorite.

After college, Casey did some work for me at Warrior, too. He went along on those sales calls with Mark and me, and he showed as much passion for partying as he did for playing lacrosse. While a guy like Mark Millon approached the game in a studious way, Casey's approach was much more laid-back. His motto was more like, "Let's just go out there and tear it up!" He was about five years younger than Mark, and he was a small-town kid who hadn't seen much of the world. Casey was the ultimate free spirit—a true rebel who happened to be one of the best lacrosse players in the world.

I guess you could say that if Mark was the sure thing, Casey was the wild card.

Even so, we knew we wanted Casey to be a part of Major League Lacrosse, and we put him on the "Take It

Outside" poster next to Mark and another great player, John Gagliardi.

I had no doubts at all that these guys would deliver on the field. The question was, would they and the rest of our players be able to handle the obligations of being part of a professional league? Would a guy like Casey be able to buckle down and take it seriously?

That, we would just have to wait and find out.

Back in our headquarters in Secaucus, New Jersey, Dave and I were kicking it into overdrive. We knew we had to hire a top-notch staff, and particularly a great executive director. We'd heard about a guy named Gabby Roe, who was not only a lacrosse nut but who had launched a professional beach soccer league that became a success in Europe. His great-grandfather was Jack Kelly, who'd won three Olympic gold medals in rowing; his great-aunt was Grace Kelly. Raised in Philadelphia, Gabby was a tough kid who brought a wrestler's mentality to lacrosse.

We eventually offered him a job as MLL's executive director. Gabby said yes, and got right to work on an official business plan. Not to bore you too much, but the model we selected for the league is called a single-entity model. That means the league itself controls the players and the venues, and brings in owner-operators to invest money for the privilege of running a team. These guys own a piece of the league, as opposed to owning their team. (Major League Soccer, for instance, operates this way.)

The single-entity model allowed us to contain and control costs. And more than anything, it was an insurance policy that everyone involved would put the interests of the league first, and their own interests second.

Then, as Dave and I continued our crazy search for investors, and as Gabby and our very small staff of two hammered out an 80-page business plan, we came to another important decision.

For a while, we considered launching the league in 2000, just a few months after our press conference. But the more work we did, the more we realized there was no reason to rush the league into existence. Yeah, we all wanted to start playing games as soon as we could, but it was much more important to get everything right— remember, we only had one shot at making this happen.

What's more, we didn't have any owner-operators in place yet. What we *did* have were the world's best players, ready to suit up and fire away.

That's when it occurred to us: Before we actually start the league, why don't we put our best asset—the players—on display? Why don't we give the world a taste of what we have in store for them? Why don't we show investors some great lacrosse, rather than just tell them about it?

Why not put on a barnstorming tour and strut our stuff?

That's what we decided to do—play a series of games in 2000 featuring the world's best players. We'd divide them into two teams, the Americans and the Nationals; we'd take them on a six-city tour; and we'd heavily market the games and get everyone adrenalized about the league. Then we could gauge fan interest, make mistakes and correct them, and show potential investors numbers and results. We'd pick cities where we knew lacrosse was hot, and a couple of markets where the game was just popping.

Most important, we'd introduce everyone to our brand of lacrosse—fast, hard-hitting, full of action. We knew most people in America weren't familiar with the sport, yet that's where we saw the opportunity. We figured if we could just get them through the gates to watch one game, we could hook them.

So we felt great about our decision, and we started gearing up for our six-city tour. We called it the Summer Showcase 2000.

We were finally ready to *take it outside.*

○

There was just this one other tiny little thing we had to do before we hit the road. Nothing major, mind you, just a small—how should I put it?—adjustment. Our goal was always to stage the most dynamic, compelling lacrosse games we could possibly stage—short of digging moats in the field and shooting flames at the players like Gladiator Guy suggested. With that in mind, I had a crazy idea, which

I immediately ran by Dave. Together, we came to a decision that a few lacrosse purists—okay, *every* lacrosse purist—basically called insane. But we went ahead with it anyway.

What did we do? We took a sport that's been around for hundreds of years and changed a couple of the rules.

You got a problem with that?

8

Lacrosse is a graceful and elegant game that combines the best elements of a lot of America's favorite sports. It's a cross between hockey (the sticks, the fast pace), soccer (teamwork, strategy, open-field dynamics), basketball (fast breaks, transition offense, goal scoring), and football (plenty of physical contact).

It's got everything Americans love about sports: hitting, scoring, and speed. So why hasn't it been more popular?

Good question.

In fact, lacrosse has been around a whole lot longer than football, baseball, or basketball—it's the oldest American sport of them all. By some accounts, a version of it was first played more than nine centuries ago, but certainly there are documents that describe it being played in North America way back in the 17th century. Native Americans engaged in fierce and often deadly lacrosse battles that spread out over many miles and lasted for days. These contests were steeped in ritual and ceremony, and were often intended to settle disputes and bring honor and glory to a tribe. French Jesuit missionaries who came to North America in the 1600s described some of these battles in their writings, and the French word for stick—*la crosse*—likely gave the sport its name.

Obviously, a lot about lacrosse has changed over the centuries, but the basics of the sport have remained pretty constant. The most important rule is that (unlike football, baseball, and basketball) you can't touch the lacrosse ball with your hands. Instead, the hard rubber ball is tossed around with sticks that have small nets on one end. In outdoor lacrosse, two teams of ten players each compete on a field that is roughly the size of a football field. The idea is to shoot the ball into a six-by-six-foot goal guarded by the opposing team's goalie. Whichever team scores the most goals wins.

The simplicity and beauty of lacrosse helps explain why it's endured for centuries. But the question remains: why hasn't it been more popular?

For a long time it was played mainly in certain hotbed areas of the United States, specifically in the Northeast. These were the places where the game originated, and it continued to flourish in prep schools, high schools, and colleges in those regions. Yet it never really caught on in other parts of the country, and most people thought of lacrosse as a game played mainly by East Coast prep-school kids.

That was one of the biggest challenges Dave and I faced when we set out to start a pro lacrosse league: How do we change the perception of lacrosse as a fringe sport? How do we take the oldest sport in America and make it seem fresh and new?

We knew we had to take the best things about lacrosse—speed, excitement, action—and make them even more appealing to a new generation of young players and fans. We had to present a version of the game that was aggressive, dynamic, and modern.

So we decided to make a couple of changes.

One of the first things we did was have Dave get to work on creating new lacrosse uniforms. The jerseys used by college teams were bulky and boring. We wanted our uniforms to be sleek and modern and cool, like the gear worn by extreme athletes. So Dave designed some very sporty Warrior jerseys.

Next, we wanted to make sure all our games were fast-paced and high scoring. In college lacrosse, if a team had a one- or two-goal lead late in a game, the players could throw the ball around without trying to score just to kill the clock. And all that stalling doesn't make for real excitement.

That's why I came up with a shot clock.

Basically, with a shot clock players have a certain amount of time to get a shot off, and if they don't, they forfeit the ball. A shot clock ensures a quick pace of play and the opportunity for plenty of scoring. I thought it would make a great addition for the sport of lacrosse.

Then I had another idea, which was inspired by my love of basketball. Goals in lacrosse have always counted for just one point. But what if we had a line on the field, and if you scored from behind that line you got two points? The NBA has a three-point line—what if we added a two-point line? A two-point shot would force defenders to follow a shooter farther away from the goal, which would create more room around the net—and lead to more exciting goal scoring.

But it would also create more games that go down to the wire. With no two-point shots, a team that is trailing by two or three goals with a minute to play is pretty much out of it—fans can pack up and head for the parking lot. But with a two-point goal, almost no lead is safe. A couple of quick two-pointers and you're back in it. In our league, no game would be over until it was over.

We would call that shot "the Deuce."

The first thing I did was run the ideas past Dave. If he had objected to changing the rules, I probably would have let it drop. When it came to lacrosse, his integrity was unquestionable and his opinion carried a lot of weight. In the end, though, Dave loved the changes.

So we fooled around with different lengths of time for our shot clock and finally settled on 45 seconds (it later became 60 seconds). And we experimented with different distances for our two-point arc, and picked 15 yards (that later became 16 yards). We really believed these changes would speed up play and make the game even more exciting for fans.

Let me tell you, when we announced the new rules, we got *killed*.

The old-school lacrosse community went nuts. They felt we were ruining a sport that had basically gone unchanged for centuries. And the fact that I was an outsider didn't help one bit. Lacrosse purists everywhere weighed in and totally trashed us. They said our league would be a circus with sticks.

But we stuck to our guns. We believed the changes weren't all that radical, and the game would look and feel the same—only it would be faster and more exciting.

Still, I didn't know for sure if we were doing the right thing until the day we finally painted a field with the new two-point arc and got the world's best players out there.

The first thing they did was go over to the two-point arc and take a shot.

I stood on the sideline watching as, one by one, the players all got behind the line and fired away. It was like watching a bunch of kids open Christmas presents. These guys were *juiced* by the two-point arc and couldn't wait to give it a go. I knew then and there we were onto something.

Even so, getting pummeled by your critics isn't fun. I mean, all we wanted to do was to grow the game and make it more popular. So why didn't the purists want us to succeed? In the months before we launched our Summer Showcase, I became a junior-varsity sports historian, reading up on the early years of all the other leagues. I saw how they all developed and evolved, trying out different rules and experimenting with new concepts.

Look at baseball in the early 1900s. They call that the "dead-ball era" because those early players were scratching out one or two runs a game. It wasn't until Babe Ruth came along in the 1920s and started hitting the long ball that baseball became the major sport it is today. So I knew every league had its growing pains, and we would be no exception.

The more those lacrosse old-schoolers killed us, the more passionate Dave and I felt about making our league happen. I mean, all that negativity just *fueled* us. It brought us closer together and gave us a trench-warfare mentality. The more convinced they were that our league would fail, the more determined we were to prove them wrong.

Of course, in order to do that we had to make sure America could *see* the game we were playing.

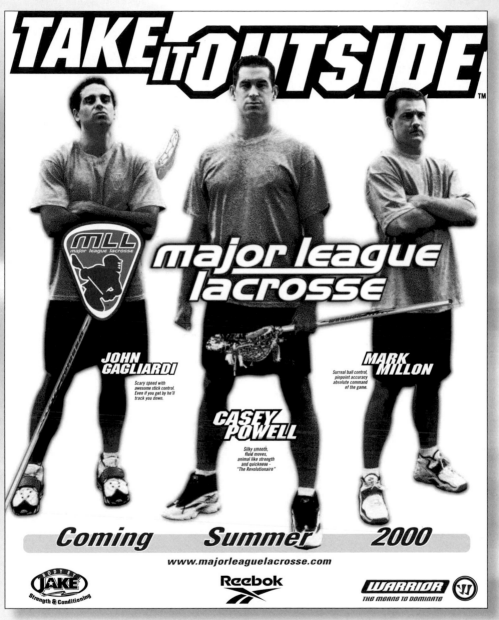

The original poster promoting Major League Lacrosse's Summer Showcase in 2000.
Boy, these guys look tough.

How many guys does it take to water a lawn? That's me, our executive director Gabby Roe, and Bridgeport Barrage co-owner Ken Paul (KP), watering the turf we just laid over the infield at Bluefish Stadium in Bridgeport, CT, in 2001.

Here I am with my pal John Kennedy, Jr., at an event honoring our friend David Pecker in New York City.

Back in 2000, I thanked the players for coming out to our first combine in Orlando and got them all fired up about our vision for MLL.

The press conference announcing the official launch of Major League Lacrosse at the Hudson Hotel in New York City in 2001. This was the biggest press conference the sport had ever seen (and by the way, no jelly donuts were served).

Pick out the fashion mogul. Certainly not me . . . maybe Dave Morrow . . . but definitely the guy in the middle, David Lauren (son of Ralph and creator of *Swing* magazine), with us at our press conference in 2001.

The Dynamic Duo! Here's Dave Morrow and me at the MLL press conference in 2001.

Here I am with the members of the Boston Cannons, one of our original teams, at our 2001 press conference: Mike Battista, Mitch Whiteley, Matt Dwyer, Peter Fahey, and David Gross (who is now MLL's commissioner).

From the Bridgeport Barrage: Ted Garber, Roy Colsey, Ken Paul, Charlie Dowd, and Mickey Herbert.

From the Baltimore Bayhawks: Mark Millon, Dave Pivec, Brian Voelker, Ray Schulmeyer, Chris Hutchins, and Gordon Boone.

From the Long Island Lizards: John DeTommaso, Casey Powell, Joe DeSimone, and Bill Bishop.

From the Rochester Rattlers: Guy Van Arsdale, Ryan Powell, Chris Economides, and Steve Donner.

From the New Jersey Pride: Jesse Hubbard, Bob Turco, and John Flood.

Just rang the closing bell at the New York Stock Exchange on Wall Street in 2001. What a rush!

Me and my gorgeous wife, Tracey.

Here's Dave and his beautiful wife, Christine.

Here I am with Connecticut Governor John Rowland, signing a proclamation that declared a statewide Major League Lacrosse weekend in 2001.

The Three Amigos (Dave Morrow, Tim Robertson, and me) with Art Modell, owner of the NFL's Baltimore Ravens.

Yeah, that's me again with the microphone (what's new?). Dave and I are presenting the Steinfeld Trophy to Long Island Lizards coach John DeTommaso (left) and an MVP check to Lizards player Gary Gait (in uniform) after their Season One championship in 2001.

MAJOR LEAGUE LACROSSE

FUEL

ALL THINGS LACROSSE

PREMIERE ISSUE

V1 I1, 06-2001

Revved & Ready

Major League Lacrosse Explodes on the Scene

HIGH OCTANE

www.majorleaguelacrosse.com

$5.00 / US

Powell Factor
An All-American Lacrosse Family

Player Secrets Revealed
Get Your Game to the MLL Level

Two Minutes and Change with Jesse Hubbard

LEAGUE AND TEAM
PREVIEWS INSIDE

The fellas are looking pretty sporty on
the cover of our first issue of *FUEL* magazine. That's me,
Dave Morrow, and Michael Watson (inside the 550 Maranello Ferrari).

Me and Dave presenting the Steinfeld Trophy at the end of another great season of MLL.
If you look closely, you can see Tim Robertson (T-Man) and his lovely wife, Lisa, behind us!

You see, another big challenge Dave and I faced was that one of the great strengths of lacrosse—its speed—was also a drawback. Pro lacrosse players can shoot the ball at around 100 mph, and that's just too fast to be picked up cleanly by TV cameras. It's the same challenge professional hockey has—following the puck on the ice can be tricky.

So a couple of months before we launched our Summer Showcase, I read an article about this guy Bill Squadron who ran a company called Sportsvision. These were the guys who came up with the illuminated first-down line for the NFL. So I picked up the phone—remember Dialing for Dollars?—and called Bill. I told him about my idea for making lacrosse easier to follow on TV by lighting up the head of the lacrosse stick whenever the ball was in it, so the television audience could easily tell who had the ball.

Bill said he loved the idea and probably could come up with technology that would cost us in the mid–seven figures.

I picked my jaw up off the floor and said, "How about the mid–*four* figures?"

The cold, hard fact was that we didn't have millions of dollars to invest in a tracking technology, or anything else for that matter. Illuminating the sticks was a good idea, just a little ahead of its time. But I never gave up on it, and I continued to work diligently to better the TV experience for our fans. For the moment, though, we would have to do our best with what we had to work with. The question was, would it be good enough?

Hey, some of the greatest achievements happened not because of money but because of something even more powerful—passion.

And when it came to passion, we were loaded.

○

Before we kicked off our Summer Showcase in July 2000, I knew we needed to have something every major sport has: a big-time beverage sponsor.

So I called the hottest new drink company around: SoBe.

SoBe stood for South Beach, which was the inspiration for a new line of herbal-enhanced tea and fruit drinks. At the time, destination-based beverages were popular—Arizona Iced Tea, Nantucket Nectars, stuff like that. The idea behind SoBe was to promote this edgy new brand through all kinds of guerilla marketing— old buses and bakery trucks painted with the company's black and green lizard logo, guys with big green afros giving away samples at skateboarding competitions, signing up larger-than-life, renegade-type athletes like skier Bode Miller and golfer John Daly.

SoBe also broke all the rules of beverage sales. For one thing, they didn't even explain what flavor their drinks were. Instead, they labeled one a "power" drink, another a "wisdom" drink, and so on. Industry people told them they were nuts, but they didn't care. They did no research and only hired people younger than 24, with no experience in sales.

Pretty quickly, they became a $200-million-a-year business.

I knew SoBe's founder, John Bello, from when he worked for NFL Properties, and he arranged a meeting for us with one of his top guys, Bill Bishop. I'd heard that Bill had played lacrosse in college and even set a school scoring record at Ohio Wesleyan. Plus, I knew SoBe was in business with a lot of cutting-edge sports. So I felt pretty good when I met the SoBe team in John's office in Norwalk, Connecticut. These guys were anything but suit-and-tie guys. They sat around in jeans and shorts and flip-flops, with their feet up on tables. John had guitars all over his office because he liked to play. I got up and pitched them on Major League Lacrosse.

And they were pumped.

SoBe was always looking for sports a little outside the mainstream, and particularly for interesting characters like Casey Powell. So they not only came aboard as a major sponsor, they signed Casey to his own endorsement deal. Bill Bishop agreed to a three-year deal to become MLL's official beverage, and in return we guaranteed them big exposure with signage at games and plugs over our PA system. SoBe cups, coolers, and towels would be everywhere on our sidelines.

Later on, Bill Bishop would play an even greater role in our league. But let's not get ahead of ourselves.

For now, we had a major beverage sponsor for our Summer Showcase. Then we snagged another big sponsor: Yahoo! Sports, a huge national website launched in 1997. Between SoBe and Yahoo! Sports, I felt that our league had taken a giant step forward. We were primed to present some top-notch lacrosse.

Now all we needed were some TV cameras to catch the action.

Timing-wise, we were pretty lucky when it came to TV coverage. There were a couple of relatively new networks that were always looking for fresh content. ESPN, the premier sports network, had launched a second channel, ESPN2, in 1993. It featured a lot of alternative sports like snowboarding and beach volleyball. I felt like we had a real shot to get ESPN2 to cover our Summer Showcase.

There was also Fox Sports Net, which debuted in 1996 and was constantly hungry for new programming as well. So I called David Hill at Fox Sports, a guy I've known since the early 1980s.

I also called my old pal Steve Bornstein, who at the time ran ESPN. I knew him from when *Body by Jake* aired on his network. David and Steve are, put simply, the two smartest guys in the sports business. I pitched the league to both of them, hoping that they'd have enough faith in me to take a chance on lacrosse. And they did. Both of them. ESPN2 would televise three of our games, and Fox Sports Net would do the other three.

We were in business.

Now it was time to pick the cities we would hit with our Summer Showcase. I left that largely to Dave, since the guy is a genius when it comes to lacrosse. No one is smarter or has a better gut when it comes to the sport. If there's a guy with a pulse holding a lacrosse stick somewhere, Dave will find him. He knew which cities were huge markets for Warrior, and he knew which areas were up-and-coming. He was the perfect guy to put us exactly where we needed to be. For our first game, we knew we had to make a splash, so we wanted a city that would guarantee us plenty of fans and enthusiasm. Dave's idea was to open the Showcase in Columbus, Ohio.

That's right, we were going to open right in the heart of football country.

It's true, Columbus wasn't exactly a hotbed of lacrosse. The sport that really mattered there was college football, because of perennial powerhouse Ohio State. But Dave looked at his sales numbers and saw that he sold a lot of lacrosse gear in Columbus. He knew the area had a lively fan base that would hopefully turn out for our game. Had we held our first game in an area where lacrosse was king, like Baltimore or Long Island, no one would have been all that surprised by a big turnout. But Dave's reasoning was that if we did really well in a place like Columbus, investors would feel better about our chances for success. With apologies to Ol' Blue Eyes, if we could make it in Columbus, we could make it anywhere.

So Columbus it was.

The other sites we picked were Philadelphia, Baltimore, Long Island, Buffalo, and Rochester.

Six games, six weeks, six cities. The 40 best players in the world. Major sponsors in place, TV contracts signed, all systems go.

Who's ready for some kick-ass lacrosse?

○

Our first Summer Showcase game was set for July 8. Honestly, I couldn't have been happier to finally be playing games and not just taking meetings, and I know Dave felt the same way. I was used to the corporate drill. Dave was a different story—he wasn't a "meetings" guy. At Warrior, he basically got together with suppliers, told them what he needed, signed a deal, and walked away. His business was very transactional.

With our league, we took a lot of meetings that went nowhere. By the time the Summer Showcase rolled around, I'm guessing we had been involved in more than 100 meetings—some boring, some strange, some just outright insane. I could tell it was wearing on both of us, Dave in particular. All those discussions about sponsorship deals and TV rights didn't really interest or engage him.

But now we were doing something Dave lived for: we were getting guys together to play lacrosse.

To get myself from New York to Ohio, I chartered a jet. I invited Dave and the Powell brothers, Casey and Ryan—who were both playing in the showcase—to come with me and my family. It was Dave's first time ever on a private jet. I soon noticed that it was Casey's first time, too.

Like Dave said, Casey was from a really tiny town in upstate New York. He hadn't seen much of the world, and I think he only owned one suit—an Armani number Dave bought for him before the Summer Showcase. So when he boarded our jet in his new suit, I couldn't resist busting his chops.

"Hey, you clean up pretty good," I told him.

Well, toward the end of the trip I noticed that Casey had gotten really quiet. He was rocking back and forth in his seat, and his face was gray. Our marquee player looked like he was going to lapse into a coma before we even landed.

"Casey, are you okay, buddy?" I asked.

"I'm all right, just nervous," he said. "*Really* nervous."

He wasn't nervous about flying. He was nervous about playing in the game. This four-time All-American was worried about how he'd play in our Showcase game.

Time for a little pep talk.

"Nervous?" I said. "You? Casey, you *own* this sport. Everyone else is worried about how they'll stack up to you out there. You're the king of this game, buddy. You're *Babe Ruth!*"

Yet that, Casey told me, was exactly why he was nervous— he didn't know if he could live up to our expectations.

"You and Dave have built me up to be this legend," Casey said. "You've been marketing me as some kind of lacrosse god. And that's great, but now I have to go out there and play like a god. And if I don't, I'll become a joke."

I was amazed by how vulnerable and human Casey was in that moment. I guess we're all so used to watching star athletes do amazing things that we forget they are regular people, just like us, with fears and insecurities. I mean, Casey was a *tremendous* lacrosse player, and here he was worried that he might not be. It reminded me our league wasn't just a collection of players.

It was a collection of people.

I assured Casey that he would play great, and I was happy to see some color return to his face once we touched down. I admit I got a little worried that one of our biggest stars might be coming down with stage fright. The one thing we knew we could count on was the quality of play in our league. But we needed our best players to play great, and if that didn't happen, well . . . I didn't even want to think about it.

We landed in Columbus a few days ahead of the first game, so we could get started marketing the Showcase. I did as many TV, radio, and newspaper interviews as I could pack into my schedule. I mean, I was all over the place, a one-man multimedia assault team. I would have worn a sandwich board and sold bratwurst and beer outside the stadium if I thought it would help us pack the place.

Thanks to all that media, and a pretty devoted fan base in Columbus, early ticket sales were great. We were playing the game at Columbus Crew Stadium, the first stadium ever designed specifically for soccer—which made it perfect for lacrosse. My pal Lamar Hunt—whom I got to know from my NFL fitness-break experience—was one of the founders of Major League Soccer, and I persuaded him to let us use Crew Stadium for our first Showcase game. It sat 20,000, but we were hoping to draw around 5,000 fans.

Everything was looking great. The only thing that could mess us up was our old familiar enemy: rain.

Which, when I looked at the newspaper, was exactly the forecast. Rain, with a chance of rain, giving way to more rain.

You've gotta be kidding, I thought to myself. *All those meetings, all that work, and now it's gonna rain on our first game?* I knew the time had come for drastic action. I had to take extraordinary steps to make sure it didn't rain.

That's when I broke out the Hawaiian shirt.

I owned this bright-orange Hawaiian shirt that I once thought looked pretty good on me. But from the stares I got, it became clear that it wasn't the greatest fashion choice I'd ever made. In fact, if I'm honest about it, that shirt looked radioactive. Nevertheless, I packed it for our trip to Columbus.

When I saw the forecast called for rain, I started thinking that if I wore the nastiest, loudest shirt I owned, I could keep the rain away. Don't ask me why I believed that, I just did. Besides, no one had a better idea. So I wore the shirt.

And guess what? It didn't rain.

I ended up wearing a wacky Hawaiian shirt to every Showcase game. Who cares if some people still think I have weird taste in menswear? I know better than to mess with a good thing.

A couple of hours before game time, we were running around making sure that everything was good to go. We had a real spectacle planned for the fans. We'd flown in professional cheerleaders from around the country, and they were ready in their short skirts and pom-poms to put on a great show. We had loudspeakers set up and aimed at the stands to pipe in rock music in between plays. And we had a whole bunch of SoBe swag to throw into the crowd—hats, towels, T-shirts, water bottles. We were ready to give our fans their money's worth, and then some.

Then it was time for me to fire up the players. We had two teams of 20 players each, the Americans and the Nationals. First I went into the Americans' locker room and gave the fellas a little pep talk. I told them this was the first step on an amazing journey. I told them they were going to be heroes in the eyes of all those kids in the stands. I told them we were on the verge of making lacrosse history.

Then I said, "Man, those guys on the Nationals are really talking smack about you. They're saying they're gonna give you guys a beatin'."

Then I went into the Nationals' locker room and said, "Boy, those are some cocky guys over there on the Americans squad. All they're talking about is how they're going to knock you guys silly on national television."

Hey, all these players deeply loved the game, and they were going to put on a great show no matter what. But now they all had their game faces on. Suddenly, it was serious. Mission accomplished.

Then Dave and I walked up to the top of the stands to get an overview of our creation.

We were looking out over the parking lot, watching cars streaming in. I mean, car after car, filling the lot, everyone coming to see what we created. It was incredible. We saw all kinds of people—young and old, men and women, families with kids carrying their lacrosse sticks. Dave and I just stood there for a few minutes, taking it all in.

"Despite everything we've been through," I said, "our dream is really happening, buddy."

"Yeah, it is," Dave said. "It really is."

Man, what a moment that was.

Then it was time to get down to business. The players were finished with their warm-ups. The fans were all in their seats on one side of the stadium, so the place would look packed on TV. Tim, Dave, and I were down on the sidelines, ready for the opening face-off. The clock ticked down the final minutes before game time.

Then the players took their positions. The ref got ready to blow the whistle for the opening face-off. The fans were on their feet cheering. No more meetings. No more crazy investors. This was it. This was finally it. It was time for Summer Showcase 2000. We were about to make history.

Ladies and gentlemen, it's showtime!

And then . . . nothing.

No face-off. No action. Just—nothing.

A couple of seconds before the ref blew the whistle, another ref stopped the action. Everyone stood around, wondering what was happening. Our executive director, Gabby Roe, ran up to me on the sidelines and said, "We can't start the game yet."

"What?" I said. "Why not?"

"We put all the fans on the side of the stadium with the sun behind them," Gabby said. "And until the sun sets, the cameras will be shooting into the glare. We won't see anything. So we have to wait for the sun to go down."

"How long is that gonna take?" I asked.

"Twenty minutes?" Gabby said hopefully.

What? Our very first game, and we're going to start 20 minutes late?

Turns out we did a walk-through with the TV people earlier that day, but no one remembered we'd be starting the game just as the sun was going down.

In fact, that long a delay was a real problem. Our players were all warmed up and ready to go, and now they had to stand around. Not to mention the 5,000 fans, who were chomping at the bit to see some real action. We couldn't very well ask 5,000 people to get up and move to the other side of the stadium. And we couldn't ask the sun to hurry up and set.

So we just had to wait.

To keep the crowd from turning on us, we pumped up the music and reintroduced the cheerleaders. Man, did they look great. The girls were jumping around like you couldn't believe.

Then the crowd started booing. They booed the cheerleaders!

I mean, they were really laying into them. These girls were all professionals; some of them were even cheerleaders for NFL teams. But the booing got so bad the girls ran off the field in tears.

Our happy, bubbly cheerleaders were sobbing!

It's not that our fans were mean or anything, it's just that they were ready for Major League Lacrosse action. Yet the sun was still up, so we couldn't give it to them.

Then we tried to put the music on louder. Maybe if the music was loud enough, they would forget about the game for a few minutes. But apparently the volume was way too loud. People started screaming, "Turn it down!" and "Shut it off!" Once again, these fans didn't want rock music. They just wanted lacrosse.

Things were going downhill fast.

We looked over at Gabby to see if we could start. He was looking at the TV guys to see if we could start. And everyone was looking at their watches, wondering when we could start.

Then the chanting started.

"WE WANT THE GAME! WE WANT THE GAME!"

Dave turned to me on the sidelines. He looked like a teenager who'd just crashed his dad's car. "Jake, what are we going to do?" he asked.

I had no answer. But then I got an idea. *The swag!*

I ran over to where we had our league bags filled with SoBe swag. Our plan was to pass this stuff out during halftime, but now we couldn't wait. I grabbed a big bag of SoBe T-shirts and started running up and down the sideline, throwing them into the stands. I was like a Roman master of ceremonies tossing hunks of bread to an angry mob in between gladiator bouts. The fans loved it, cheering wildly and trying to get their hands on more free T-shirts.

This is working, I thought.

Then I ran out of swag. And the sun still hadn't dropped behind the stadium walls.

I went back for another bag, this one filled with SoBe towels. I emptied that one, too. I looked at the sun. Nope, still there. What was this—a watched sun never sets? I looked over at Gabby, and he gave me a look that said, "Almost, Jake! Almost!" Gee, that was helpful.

I went back for another bag, this one filled with SoBe caps. They weren't easy to hurl into the stands, but eventually I got them all up there.

Then I looked at the sun again. *Still* there.

"Hey Dave, throw me another bag of this stuff," I said. "One more bag ought to do it."

"Jake, there are no more bags," Dave said. "You just gave away all the SoBe stuff we had—*for the whole Summer Showcase.*"

Oops.

I looked over at the sun, and finally, it was gone.

At last, we were ready to play. But there was another problem.

Earlier in the day, Dave and I met up with the Crew Stadium's public address announcer. This was the guy who was going to call the game in the stadium. He introduced himself as "the Voice of the Columbus Crew for Major League Soccer," and he told us he'd been handling a lot of soccer broadcasts.

"That's great," I said, "but just remember, this is lacrosse. Sticks and helmets, okay?"

"No problem," said the Voice, and we went away figuring he could handle the transition from soccer to lacrosse.

We figured wrong.

Up in the broadcast booth, the Voice kicked off the festivities by saying, "Welcome to Major League Soccer!"

I looked at Dave. "Did he just say Major League *Soccer?*"

Dave just shook his head.

Just two minutes later, the Voice boomed, "Major League Soccer is pleased to welcome all of you fans!"

"Please tell me this moron didn't say soccer again."

Dave didn't even acknowledge me. He knew if I got too worked up I might do something crazy.

A couple of minutes later, the Voice got a player's name wrong, and then his uniform number wrong, and then another player's name wrong, and on and on. Let me have Dave pick up the story from here:

The first time the Voice accidentally said soccer, I chuckled nervously. The second time, I looked away from Jake because I was worried he would run up to the booth and toss this guy out the window. Then when the Voice started messing up names and numbers, Tim Robertson pulled me over and said, "Check out Jake—there's smoke coming out of his ears."

But by the time I looked over at Jake, he was gone.

I didn't know where he had gone, and I didn't want to know. I found out soon enough, though, when I heard a familiar voice over the PA system.

"Well, folks, whaddya think of Major League *Lacrosse* so far?"

The first thing I did was look for the Voice's body on the field. No evidence of a corpse. So that was good.

I later learned that Jake had rounded up a security guard and made a mad dash for the broadcast booth. By the time he got there, his orange Hawaiian shirt was soaked through with sweat. I presume he was frothing at the mouth. He stood in the doorway and said two words to the Voice: "You're done."

The Voice was stunned, and pleaded his case, to no avail.

"This is Major League Lacrosse, not soccer, and I'm taking over," Jake said. "Just tell me which buttons to press."

So Jake called the rest of the game, cheering on great plays and marveling at amazing goals just like any other fan. The crowd just ate it up. At that moment I realized Jake was the Flash. He was everywhere, all the time, doing whatever needed to be done. Okay, he was like the Flash moonlighting as a Barnum & Bailey ringmaster.

I'm not good around crowds. But to Jake, crowds were a power source, there for him to plug into and get super amped. When things went haywire, he didn't stand around cursing our bad luck. He did whatever was needed to turn that luck around. He was the league's founder, head cheerleader, and play-by-play guy all rolled into one. And that hideous Hawaiian shirt! On most people it would have looked absolutely ridiculous. But on Jake, somehow, it didn't look half bad.

That game was a real eye-opener for me. I was learning another lesson from Jake. The thing he always says is that life is about moments, and that first game was one of those moments. And Jake didn't shrink away from it—he rose to it. He rose to the moment. He was showing me what it takes to be truly successful.

What it takes is everything you've got.

Hey, I never intended to call the game, but once I was up in that booth I had a blast. I made sure the fans had a blast, too.

After all those early screwups, everything turned out to be great. We sent the cheerleaders out to the field again in between plays, and although they got booed again, it wasn't nearly as bad. Before long, the booing stopped altogether. So that saved us a couple of grand in therapy sessions for the ladies.

And the game itself? Man, it was great. Lots of action, lots of scoring, lots of incredible goals. In the end it was a barn burner, with the Nationals winning 23–21.

As for Casey Powell, he played beautifully. Once he got on the field, all the nervousness went away. With a lacrosse stick in his hand, the kid is an artist. He sure created a real work of art that day.

Game One of our Summer Showcase was over. The fans streamed down to the field, happy as clams. All of our players stuck around and signed autographs until every last kid was safely tucked away in the back of an SUV. Everyone told us how great it was to be able to see these players play. We all had a real feeling of accomplishment, and we couldn't wait for Game Two in Philadelphia. I packed up my trusty Hawaiian shirt and hoped that we'd worked out all the kinks with Game One.

That, my friends, is what you call wishful thinking.

The traveling carnival that was our Summer Showcase invaded Philadelphia for Game Two. Just as I had in Columbus, I spent the days before the game hammering home our message. I did every radio show, every sports program, every "Live at 5," every local paper— anyone who would listen, I talked to. And what I told them was always the same. "One day kids will have a poster of their favorite MLL player hanging on their bedroom wall next to their favorite NBA or NFL players," I said in one interview. "These guys play with such passion that it is instantly contagious, and if you aren't a lacrosse fan when you arrive at the stadium, you certainly will go home one."

As game day approached, Dave and I watched the broadcast of the first game in Columbus. We were learning on the fly, and obviously we made a few mistakes—like hiring an announcer who couldn't tell soccer from lacrosse, and pointing our cameras directly at the sun. So we fixed what we could fix, learned from our mistakes, and moved on.

Then we went to work converting Villanova Stadium's football field into a lacrosse field. Our guys spread out, hanging SoBe signs everywhere. One of the most important things we had to do was make sure our sponsors had maximum exposure. So let me tell you, we had SoBe signs in just about every nook and cranny of that stadium. We might make other mistakes that night, but at least our major sponsor was going to be happy, right?

Wrong.

The signs had to come down.

No sooner had our guys draped the place with SoBe signs than some Villanova reps came running out, waving for them to stop. "We're sorry, but we have an exclusive agreement with another major beverage company," they said. "We can't allow any other soft drink to be advertised or marketed in the stadium."

Whoa, hold it. This was a disaster. We were lucky enough to have SoBe on board, but now we couldn't feature their name anywhere in the telecast?

Gabby, our executive director, argued with the stadium management staff for a while before enlisting my help. "Jake, these guys aren't bending," he said. "They say no SoBe signs will be allowed. What are we going to do?"

"Let me talk to them," I said.

I found Villanova's athletic director and tried to reason with him. "How about I make a nice donation to the athletic department?" I asked. "I'll write you a check, or we'll have Dave donate all the lacrosse sticks you need."

"Sorry, Jake," the AD said. "We can't violate our contract."

And that was that—no SoBe signs.

Turns out none of our guys checked with the stadium crew ahead of time about any competing sponsor agreement.

Rookie mistake.

Now I had to call John Bello, co-founder of SoBe, and tell him the one thing we were contractually bound to give him—exposure at our games—just wasn't going to happen. I told John that we would do whatever we had to in order to make it up to SoBe, and to his great credit, John didn't get bent out of shape. He was a real pro who understood the world of sports marketing. He even thanked me for being so honest. Still, I felt rotten about it.

But at least we got our one major snafu out of the way before game time, right?

Wrong again.

On the afternoon of the game, Gabby came running up to me again. "Jake, you gotta talk to the ESPN guy," he said.

Next thing I know, I'm standing on the 40-yard line with an ESPN producer, and he's telling me we don't have enough "candlepower" to televise the game.

Candlepower?

Basically, by game time the level of light intensity in the stadium wouldn't be strong enough to create a good televised image. "The candlepower in this stadium isn't great," the ESPN guy said. "The TV audience won't be able to follow the action."

"Okay, fine. What do we need to make it work?"

"Well, one additional lighting package would help, but to create a truly professional sports broadcast, you need two more packages."

"And what's that gonna cost?" I asked, expecting to cringe.

"Thirty thousand dollars," he told me.

I didn't cringe. I convulsed.

"Thirty grand?" I said. "What are we, lighting up downtown Philly?" By the way, that was just the cost of a two-hour *rental.* Once again, our guys forgot to make sure the lighting system in Villanova was powerful enough for TV.

Another rookie mistake.

"Can't we make it work with the lights that are already there?" I pleaded. "Or maybe just one extra light package?"

"Jake, it's up to you," the ESPN producer said. "Are you pro, or are you junior varsity?"

I knew the answer to that question, but I still had to take a step back and think about what to do. You have to understand, we were operating under the tightest budget imaginable. In terms of game-day expenses, we barely had two lacrosse sticks to rub together. So when they told us we had to come up with an extra *$30,000,* it hurt, man. It felt like we were being hijacked.

It was one of those moments when you start to wonder, *What in the world did we get ourselves into?*

I got ahold of Dave, and we put in a conference call to Tim Robertson in Virginia. Of the three of us, Tim was the disciplined money manager, so I knew he wouldn't be thrilled. I explained the situation, and we all kicked it around. Dave was right next to me, so I could tell from his stunned expression that he wasn't crazy about shelling out all that extra dough. And judging from Tim's silence, I was pretty sure he wasn't wild about the idea, either.

Yet I knew we were facing a moment of truth here. We could have said no to the extra lights and taken our chances with the broadcast. Or we could hand over the down payment on a pretty decent house.

What were we going to do?

Finally, I spoke up. "Guys, this is where our standards are put to the test," I said. "When I asked you guys to join me in this deal, I told you we would never do anything halfway. I said we would be a major league in every sense of the word. It's like the producer said: do you want to be junior varsity, or do you want be pro?"

In the end, we cut the check.

I ran down and went up to the rig with the lighting package on it, and I hugged that thing like it was my long-lost brother. I still have a picture of me with my arms around those $30,000 babies. In fact, I held on to it for so long someone had to finally tell me to let go. Hey, for 30 grand I should have been able to take that thing to dinner and a movie.

But now, at least, we had our lights. The game was going to look great. Another crisis averted. What else could go wrong?

How about rain? That's right, with all the fans already in the stadium, the skies opened up.

It doesn't matter how much candlepower you have, rain makes any telecast look washed out. Did we just spend 30 large for nothing? I stood in the downpour and wondered if MLL stood for "Murphy's Law Lacrosse."

Yet I didn't lose all hope, because I had a secret weapon: my Hawaiian shirt.

If I was wearing it, the rain would have to stop, right? Well, it did—eventually.

We had 5,109 fans show up for Game Two. Right before face-off, I ran out to midfield with a microphone and thanked everyone for coming. It was another great contest, with the Americans winning 17–12. Afterward, our players mingled with the fans and signed autographs for every last kid. I'm sure we would have basked in that moment if we hadn't felt so drained. The games themselves were great, but all the mistakes and unexpected setbacks were really wearing us down.

And guess what? We still had four games to go.

○

Believe it or not, everything kind of settled down for Game Three in Baltimore. We were set up at UMBC Stadium on the beautiful campus of the University of Maryland, Baltimore County. The place sat around 5,000, and we were hoping for a sellout. It's a field that's used for both soccer and lacrosse, so we didn't have to do much to get it ready.

We could also hang our SoBe signs wherever we wanted.

The night before the game, I draped my Hawaiian shirt on a chair in my hotel room and pointed it at the window, to ward off the rain gods. Hawaiian shirts were quickly becoming my lucky charm— and my sartorial signature. During the Summer Showcase I wore one everywhere, and people would constantly call out, "Hey, Jake, love the shirt!" I became the Versace of palm trees and pineapples. And as long as they kept working, I'd keep wearing them.

In Baltimore, it worked again—perfect weather.

I drove to the stadium with my wife, Tracey; and our kids, Morgan, Nick, and Zach. UMBC Stadium sits on a little hill, and before the game Dave, Tim, and I went up to the top of that hill and stood near the entrance. Then we just waited. We knew how hard it had been just to get to this point, and we wanted to enjoy the moment.

We wanted to see all the fans.

They came, by the thousands. Seeing all those people come together to enjoy something we had created was incredibly satisfying. We had a VIP tent, and it was buzzing with activity. There were food tents, and the delicious smell of crab cakes was wafting through the air. We had an awesome summer evening . . . thanks, of course, to my shirt. It felt like we were at a really big, really festive clambake—with some amazing lacrosse thrown in as a bonus.

That game in Baltimore had it all going. The first two games were thrilling, sure, but there had been so many foul-ups and crises that we couldn't really enjoy what we'd accomplished. But up on that hill, watching a few thousand fans stream past us into the stadium, we all finally took a breath and allowed ourselves to feel pride in what we'd done. We had created something that didn't exist, and people were excited about it. On that one night anyway, everything was perfect.

I remember standing there, thinking, *This is Major League Lacrosse.* In the end, we drew 5,513 fans. The place was jammed.

But there wasn't time for celebrating. As soon as Game Three ended, we had to get ready for our next stop. And this one was a big one, at least for me. Our next game would be played in Long Island, New York.

My hometown.

The chubby kid with the stutter was coming home, and he was bringing his new friends with him.

○

Needless to say, I really wanted Game Four of the Summer Showcase to go great. We were playing in the Mitchel Athletic Complex in Uniondale, Long Island, which was just over the Southern State Parkway from where I grew up. I did an enormous amount of press, even more than usual. The big local paper, *Newsday,* did a huge write-up on me and the Summer Showcase. It seemed like everyone was genuinely pumped for the arrival of pro lacrosse on Long Island . . . everyone, that is, except the Coach.

The Coach is the name I'm giving to this one particularly opinionated critic of what we were doing. He was a semi-prominent lacrosse coach on Long Island, and I guess he considered himself a purist, because every time we turned around he was calling MLL a sham and a circus. This guy was definitely not a fan. We had plenty of critics back then—in fact, most people in the lacrosse world didn't give us much chance to succeed. But this guy was particularly vocal, and it was starting to bug us.

So you know what we did?

No, we didn't lock him in the trunk of a car. You should know me better by now.

What we did was make him our ambassador.

A couple of days before the game, I told Gabby to invite the Coach to watch us play. Gabby was a little confused, since this guy was treating us like an old bath mat. But this was my reasoning: When you're on the outside of something, it's a lot easier to rip it to shreds. But when you get invited into the fold, your opinion is going to change. Why make an enemy of this guy when we could kill him with kindness? Why not make him our ambassador?

"Yeah, but what does that even mean?" Gabby asked.

"I don't know," I said. "Why don't we just put him on the sidelines, give him an MLL jacket, you know, swag him up. I bet we can win this guy over."

The Coach accepted our invitation, and soon we'd find out if watching our players in action—and getting a little free gear—turned him from a hater to a fan.

Even so, I had a lot bigger challenges on my mind than winning over the Coach.

The day before every game, we held a full-squad workout on the field. All 40 players were required to show up and get ready to play the next day. The day before the Long Island game, I got a call in my hotel room from Gabby.

"Jake, Casey and Ryan Powell aren't at practice," he said.

I got off the phone with Gabby and immediately called Dave. The players were generally his responsibility, just as doing interviews and dealing with sponsors were mine. Dave knew these guys, and he had many of them under contract with Warrior—including both Powell brothers.

"Hey, where are the fellas?" I asked.

"I don't know," Dave said.

"Well, we've gotta go find them."

We went over to the hotel where the players were staying and headed straight for Casey's room. I banged on the door, and Casey let us in.

He and Ryan were there with a couple of girls.

Turns out the Powell brothers were partying the night before, stayed out until the wee hours, then came home with their new companions and slept right through practice. This time, smoke really *was* coming out of my ears. We politely asked the girls to go, and I turned around a desk chair and sat facing Casey and Ryan.

Then I blasted them.

I told the brothers that this was a business, and we had invested a lot of money in it and them. "You guys are being given the chance of a lifetime," I said, "so why are you acting like a couple of knuckle-noses?" I went on and on about responsibility, opportunity, and the importance of being on time. Finally, after 45 minutes, I got up and left.

I heard that afterward, Casey and Ryan sat on their beds in stunned silence for a few minutes, before Casey finally spoke.

"Wow," he said. "We just got reamed by Body by Jake."

When I was finished with the Powells, I went straight to the field at Mitchel Athletic Complex, where the other 38 players were practicing. I rounded them into a circle at midfield and gave them a speech.

"This isn't college or a lacrosse club," I said. "This isn't, 'Hey, let's get a keg of beer and toss the ball around.' This is a business. And that's how we're going to run it—as a business."

Then I told the guys about two new rules Dave and I had just made up on the ride back to the stadium: "Anyone misses a practice, you get fined and suspended for one game. You miss two practices, and you're fired. Does everyone understand?"

The players nodded their heads. But then one of them spoke up, asking, "That doesn't go for the Powell brothers, does it?"

I knew what he was saying. Casey was a star, one of our main attractions, and these guys figured I gave him more leeway. But that was not the case.

"It goes for everyone," I said. *"Everyone."*

And I meant it.

Dave and I both knew what was going on with Casey. He was a brilliant talent and a really sweet guy, but he was also only 24 and just a couple of years out of college. The only dream he'd ever had in his life was to play lacrosse at Syracuse, and once he accomplished that, he didn't really have another goal. So for him, the MLL wasn't a big deal—it was just another chance to hang out with the guys and party.

"I had already lived my dream at Syracuse, so I didn't understand the significance of what Jake and Dave were doing," Casey says now. "I was like, 'Come on, let's just go out and play.' I didn't really get the importance of it. It was a matter of having to rethink my entire situation."

That's why Dave and I constantly stressed to Casey and the others that they weren't just players—they were pioneers. They were out here blazing a trail for the next generation. We wanted them to share our vision for MLL—to look ahead 10 or 20 years and imagine themselves as the elder statesmen of a thriving league. Some people have the vision to see what isn't there, and some don't. For others, like Casey, it just takes time.

The day after my speech, both Casey and Ryan went out and played their guts out.

Game Four went really well, except for one little hiccup. Mitchel Athletic Complex had an oval running track around the field, which meant the fans were seated farther away from the action than usual. To keep them engaged and entertained, we set up big speakers and piped in music throughout the game, but people kept coming up and pleading with us to shut off the music.

Slowly but surely, we were starting to get it—we didn't need a lot of bells and whistles to make things work. The fans were coming to see great lacrosse, and we *had* that. And if you have a great steak, you're going to get the sizzle—so you don't have to try to create extra sizzle. Eventually, we realized we didn't have to dress up our games— we just had to play them.

After the game, we set up tables for the players to meet the fans and sign autographs. Not just a few of the players, but all 40 of them. There was a long line of excited kids waiting to have them sign their hats and posters and sticks. But it wasn't only kids.

This one older guy came up to me, happy and excited and waving his MLL poster like he was 12. "I just wanted to tell you, I had the time of my life," he said.

"Thank you, and spread the word," I replied. "Tell everyone about MLL."

When he left, Gabby came running up to me. "That was him!" he said.

"Who?"

"The Coach! That was the Coach!"

Our biggest hater had become our biggest fan. The Coach was now "the Ambassador."

○

We left for our next stop on a real high because of how well the Long Island game went. Now we were heading to upstate New York, a hotbed of lacrosse. We'd be playing two games in three days, in Buffalo and Rochester. The Rochester game, in particular, was going to be a real spectacle. It would be the last game of the Summer Showcase —our last hurrah before we tried to launch an actual season. And it would be held in what was basically Casey and Ryan Powell's backyard. These guys were lacrosse legends, and we expected a huge crowd to turn out to watch them play. I couldn't wait to see what happened in Rochester.

But first came Buffalo—and one of the worst moments of the entire Showcase.

We were playing in Dunn Tire Park, a baseball stadium and home to the minor-league Buffalo Bisons. One of our biggest hurdles when we started the league was finding good places to play. There weren't any true lacrosse stadiums, so much of the time we had to settle for football or baseball fields. And let me tell you, converting the fields from baseball to lacrosse was a nightmare. Half a baseball field is dirt, so we had to come in days ahead of time, re-sod the whole field, then magically turn it back into a baseball diamond when we left. It was hugely expensive, and the results were often a sloppy field.

At the time we felt we had no choice, though—we wanted to be seen as a professional league, and we felt everything had to be perfect. In hindsight, we probably didn't have to go to the trouble of re-sodding. I mean, look at the Oakland Raiders. For a long time they didn't bother converting the baseball diamond at the Oakland Coliseum, and played on a field that was half grass, half dirt— and they were always seen as an elite NFL franchise. In time, we understood that it wasn't about a great field; it was about great lacrosse. That's what fans wanted. But back then, we wanted to be taken seriously as a professional league, so we converted Dunn Tire Park into a true lacrosse venue.

The game got under way, and for two quarters everything was great. But then midway through the third quarter, something happened that we hadn't seen in the previous four games.

A fight broke out.

One of the midfielders went up in the air to catch a pass, and while he was up there, fully extended, a defender came flying in and T-boned the guy. I mean, he just laid him out. It was an illegal hit, and when the midfielder went down in a heap, his teammates jumped to his defense. Pretty soon, we had several players mixing it up at midfield. Most of the fans were cheering, but Dave and I were not.

Up until that point, we didn't have a rule against fighting. There was a rule against it in the college game, but we purposefully didn't have one because we thought our fans might like to see a little pushing and shoving. We wanted to leave some room for that kind of action.

Yet when that hit happened, everything changed. Watching the players fight and hearing the fans cheering made us realize that this wasn't what we wanted. Lacrosse is a magnificent game, so fluid and beautiful, and ugly fights take away from that. And besides, lacrosse has plenty of hitting that's legal, so you don't need any extracurricular sparring.

Luckily, the fight on the field wound down, and the game resumed. The midfielder who'd been pancaked was okay. But afterward, Dave and I made an executive decision. Major League Lacrosse would not allow fighting. We believed lacrosse was, at heart, a finesse game. People loved the speed and the scoring and, yes, the hitting— but they didn't need to see a scene from *Fight Club*.

Another crisis averted.

If only it had been the last.

○

Our final Summer Showcase game would be played at Frontier Field, another minor-league baseball park in downtown Rochester. Once again, we were hoping to draw at least 5,000 fans. We wanted to go out on a really high note, so we did everything in our power to make sure Game Six was the most exciting, most compelling Showcase game yet.

The night before, I once again draped my Hawaiian shirt on a chair in my hotel room and positioned it near the window. The next morning I pulled open the drapes, and beautiful sunlight streamed in. My kids were happily running around the room, my wife and I were enjoying breakfast, and everything just seemed perfect. This was our last game, the summer was winding down, and for one of the few times during the whole Summer Showcase, I felt a real sense of peace and calm.

Then the phone rang.

It was Gabby Roe, who told me, "Ryan Powell is not at practice."

Now, you might think news like that would have set me off. But actually I just took it in stride. I was used to last-minute disasters by then. "No problem," I told Gabby. "Ryan doesn't play. That's one less guy we have to pay."

"But, Jake," Gabby said, "if Ryan doesn't play, Casey says he won't play, either."

Okay, now *that* was a problem. We were in Rochester, just a short drive from where the legendary Powell brothers grew up. Most of the fans were coming to see them play. Plus, we had heavily promoted Casey as the Babe Ruth of lacrosse, and if both he and Ryan didn't play, how would we look?

I had a tough decision to make. Should I ignore the rule we just created and let the Powells play? Or should I stick to my guns, even if it meant disappointing our fans?

I knew what I had to do, and I did it.

"No problem," I told Gabby again. "Neither one plays."

I talked it over with Dave, expecting he might try to defend his guys. But Dave agreed with me 100 percent. We had to take a stand

and let these guys know that there were consequences if they missed a practice and didn't follow the rules. We couldn't have a league where players decided which games and which practices they would attend. The league itself had to be bigger than any one player, or else it wouldn't work.

We laid down the law: Ryan wasn't playing. And if Casey didn't want to play, that was up to him. We felt bad for the fans, but we had no choice.

Looking back, that was a turning point for the league. If we had let Ryan play, somewhere down the road the same thing would have happened again. We had to set an example right then and there. We had to show everyone involved that this was a business, and that it would be run like a business. And from that moment on, that's exactly how it's been run—like a business.

So, no Ryan Powell.

The question was: would Casey sit out in support of his brother, or would he show up and play?

Dave and I went back to getting ready for Game Six. I put on my really low-key, understated Hawaiian shirt and drove to Frontier Field. I stopped in at the TV camera truck before the game, as was my habit, to check in on my director and maybe offer a suggestion or two for a new camera angle. I also ran around greeting fans and shaking hands. Soon, I would jog out to midfield, thank the fans for coming, and get ready for the opening face-off.

Game time approached. The stands filled up. The Americans and Nationals came out for their warm-ups. Everything was looking good for our sixth and final Showcase game—except, that is, for no Ryan or Casey.

And then, shortly before game time, I looked out at the field and saw a player wearing the Nationals jersey with number 22 on his back. I recognized him right away.

Casey had decided to play.

The game got under way, and I noticed that Casey was a madman out there. He was playing his heart out and scoring left and right. The fans were going wild and cheering him on. Everyone played really well that game, but Casey played beautifully, showing off the full range of his awesome talents.

That afternoon in Rochester, Casey *was* Babe Ruth.

Meanwhile, in the tunnel leading out to Frontier Field, Casey's brother Ryan stood and watched the whole game by himself.

As the final seconds ticked off the clock, I stood in the press box and watched the fans all get up on their feet. We'd been hoping for a crowd of around 5,000—we got nearly 5,500. And here they were, every last one of them, on their feet and giving the players a standing ovation.

A spontaneous, bleacher-shaking standing O.

We didn't have an applause sign. There was no stage manager urging the fans to cheer. Not to mention the fact that the game hadn't really meant anything—it was just an exhibition.

Yet none of that mattered. What mattered was that the folks from Rochester loved great lacrosse, and they loved watching the best players in the world play it. So everyone rose up on their own and cheered wildly for about two minutes. The players took their bows and waved with their sticks and basked in their big moment.

Up in the press box, I got goose bumps. Man, my goose bumps got goose bumps.

I looked over at Dave, and he looked at me, and we didn't even have to say a word. We just smiled and shook our heads as if to say, "Can you believe this?"

All the nonsense, all the heartache, all the uncertainty, all the hard work—all of it, in that moment, was worth it.

The Summer Showcase was over.

But Major League Lacrosse was just getting started.

○

To celebrate, we planned a party at a local sports-themed bar called Jillian's. We bought three Rolex watches, and we were going to hand them out to the three Most Valuable Players—one on offense, one on defense, and one overall MVP. It was the perfect way for us to wind down and savor what we'd accomplished.

After the game, Casey came over to talk. I told him he'd played a great game, and he thanked me. Then he asked if Ryan could come to the party.

"Casey, let me ask you a question," I said. "If you got fired from a job, do you think you'd still be invited to the company Christmas party?"

Casey got the picture. I could tell he felt bad, but I could also tell he understood the decision. He realized that actions have consequences. That's why he chose to play in the game, and not sit out just because his brother got suspended.

Later that year, Ryan wound up writing me a heartfelt letter, apologizing for missing practice and telling me how bad he felt. That letter meant a lot to me. That's when I knew that the Powell brothers would continue to be involved with Major League Lacrosse for a long, long time.

The party at Jillian's was a blast. We presented the defensive MVP award to Greg Cattrano, a world-class goalie and one of our biggest stars. Then we gave the offensive MVP award to Mark Millon, whom we'd featured on our original "Take It Outside" poster.

Then it was time for the overall Summer Showcase MVP award, and the last shiny Rolex. This award was for the one player who had shined above all others, demonstrating all the great talent and artistry that our league would be built on. Dave and I consulted on the award, but the choice was obvious.

"The overall MVP award goes to . . . Casey Powell!"

Casey shuffled up, collected his spiffy new watch, and gave me a sheepish grin. I pulled him in for a monster hug.

To this day, he wears that Rolex on his wrist.

That night, Casey made the right decision. He did what was right for the league, and for himself. He stepped up and seized the moment.

And life is all about moments—remember?

After the award ceremony, Dave and I took a couple of minutes to look back on what we'd done. So many people told us we wouldn't make it out of the Summer Showcase. So many predicted we'd draw only a few busloads of fans and have to fold up shop. Yet here we were, still on our feet.

Did we have some major setbacks? We sure did. We had too much rain one day, and too much sun the next. We played our music too loud, and our cheerleaders got booed. We had an announcer who couldn't remember what sport he was covering, and we could have put a kid through a year of college for what we paid to rent lights for two hours.

We also had our share of highlights: the unforgettable first goal in Columbus, the moment on the hill in Baltimore, the thrilling enthusiasm of fans everywhere—and, of course, the great lacrosse that was played at every stop.

But when Dave and I took time to look back on those amazing six weeks, we were doing more than celebrating the past.

We were celebrating our future.

You see, we knew all along that we needed a great Summer Showcase to launch the league. We needed to see that fans were interested in our product; we needed to see big crowds and great action on the field. And we saw all those things. We confirmed that people wanted to watch professional outdoor lacrosse.

Now, all we had to do was make it work. That meant finding some really top-notch owners to run our teams. Piece of cake, right?

Or at least that's what we hoped that night at Jillian's. We had no way of knowing that our toughest times were still ahead . . . and that no Hawaiian shirt could keep those storms at bay.

One of the most memorable meetings I ever had was at the head-quarters of one of the great fashion brands, Ralph Lauren.

From the very beginning, I always thought that the Polo brand would be a perfect fit with Major League Lacrosse. Remember, I first read about Dave Morrow in *Swing* magazine, which was run by Ralph Lauren's son David. I called David early on and pitched him on having Polo become an MLL sponsor, and he loved the idea. We talked about different things we could do together, and he was always very enthusiastic. He told me to keep him posted on our progress and to call him when we got closer to launching.

He was so enthusiastic that I remember telling Dave Morrow, "I really think we're going to put a deal together here." So when we finally set up a meeting at Polo headquarters, I felt great about our chances. I even allowed myself to imagine a whole line of Ralph Lauren Lacrosse apparel, and maybe even Ralph Lauren Lacrosse stores! My mind was going a mile a minute. I told Dave I didn't need him for the meeting—I had it covered.

I flew from L.A. to New York City and walked into a beautifully appointed executive conference room in the company's Madison Avenue offices. David was there, along with several Polo people led by this dapper British fellow named Paddy, who was some kind of marketing whiz. David got up and made all the introductions, and even shared a couple of stories of our trip to Detroit with JFK, Jr. Then I got up and talked about our new lacrosse league and the sport's growing popularity, and how there was great potential for Polo Ralph Lauren in the world of lacrosse.

The pitch went great, if I may say so myself. Everyone was listening intently, nodding and taking notes. I figured all we had to do now was write up the contract and sign on the dotted line.

Not so fast, Bosco.

Before we could even get down to business, Paddy piped up. In his upper-crust English accent, he said, "You know, Jake, in England lacrosse is considered a girl's game."

I guess I just assumed Paddy was yanking my chain, like we did to each other in the old neighborhood. So I quickly delivered what I thought was a pretty clever comeback.

"Well, you know, in America, Paddy is considered a girl's name."

I chuckled as I said it, and I looked around to find that no one else was chuckling.

Especially not Paddy.

No, good old Paddy was staring daggers at me, like I'd just backed my pickup into his Jaguar.

He got up from the table, gave me one last death stare, and stormed out of the room.

"Hey, Paddy, you're kidding me, right?" I called after him. "We're just busting each other's chops, right?"

No response. Paddy was gone.

I glanced over at David Lauren. He didn't look thrilled, either. "Jake, what have you done?" he said.

"What? I thought we were joking."

"Paddy is our chief marketing officer. If he's gone, this meeting's over."

And with that, Polo's marketing people got up and left the room. David came over and tried to console me.

"I'm sorry, Jake," he said. "I think this is great, but we're gonna have to give it a little time. We'll see if we can work something out down the line."

So much for that dream of a Ralph Lauren Lacrosse store in every mall.

○

My point in telling this fairly embarrassing story is that the leadership of Major League Lacrosse wasn't exactly out of central casting. Dave Morrow and I were not your typical CEOs in Brooks Brothers suits and Burberry loafers. Dave was the long-haired rebel turning lacrosse on its head with his cutting-edge equipment company, and I was the Hollywood fitness guy. We weren't anyone's idea of a prim-and-proper management team.

But to us, that wasn't a disadvantage; it was an asset. Sure, we were different, but that was the point—our league was going to be different, too. We were creating a dynamic new version of the sport—a new game for a new century.

We'd proven to ourselves that we could do it with the Summer Showcase. But could we convince a group of successful sports businesspeople to open up their checkbooks and buy one of our teams? Could we get some guys with deep pockets to believe in our crazy dream?

Could we do a little better than I did with Paddy from Polo?

I sure hoped so.

But first, I set my sights on something that would bolster our chances with any prospective owner. It was something that would give our league instant credibility. It was something I called the Sports Legitimizer.

I went after Anheuser-Busch.

A sponsorship deal with the King of Beers was the biggest prize any sports league could hope to win. Budweiser was synonymous with sports—you couldn't watch a game of football or baseball or basketball without seeing Bud Light signage everywhere. So if we could snag Anheuser-Busch as a sponsor, I knew it would be that much easier to convince prospective owners that we were legit.

I contacted Steve Uline, the guy who directed sports marketing at Anheuser-Busch. I told him what we were doing, and he agreed to meet with me. At their office in St. Louis, Uline and his team were used to getting pitched by wacky alternative sports leagues, and most of the time they just said no. They concentrated on the top-tier leagues—the NFL, the NBA, MLB—as well as a few less mainstream sports like volleyball and surfing.

Their brand was so powerful that they could create a sport all by themselves. As a sponsor of professional rodeos, they noticed that one particular event—bull riding—was more popular and exciting than the others. So they convinced the top 45 bull riders in the country to put up $1,000 each, kicked in $45,000 of their own, and launched the Professional Bull Riders tour.

Luckily, when I came calling, Anheuser-Busch was looking for a sport that was popular in the Northeast. They had the West Coast covered with surfing and volleyball, but they were looking for a lifestyle sport that could help them appeal to men in their 20s in the northern part of the country.

Lacrosse, anyone?

Uline and his top marketing person, Kathy Casso, met with me in their office. Part of the reason they brought me in was that they knew me from my fitness shows. (See? I told you that was an asset.) They figured that at the very least, I'd keep them entertained for an hour.

I got up in front of them in a conference room and did my rap-a-doo about the league. Listen, I knew I wasn't exactly in lacrosse country. In fact, most people in St. Louis knew less than nothing about the sport at the time. But I told Steve and Kathy what I tell everyone: American sports fans love hitting, scoring, and speed, and we have them all. We have the fastest-growing game in the country.

"What size crowds are you predicting?" Steve asked.

I could have said 10,000 fans a game, but we knew from the Summer Showcase that wasn't our number. It was possible, but not likely, at least not at the start. So I told them more along the lines of 5,000 fans a game.

They asked me what kind of sponsorship deal I was looking for.

"We'll design whatever kind of plan works for you," I said.

I didn't go in and big-time these guys. I didn't throw around a lot of inflated numbers. I was passionate and optimistic, but at the same time I was pretty realistic about our goals. That was always my MO when I talked about our league. We believed we had a great product, and either people saw what we saw or they didn't.

Thank goodness, Steve and Kathy did.

They agreed to have Anheuser-Busch become an official sponsor of Major League Lacrosse. In return they got signage at games, promotional ties to one of our teams, and stuff like a Bud Light Party tent in the Fan Zone. They would also be the presenting sponsor of the league's MVP award.

To have Anheuser-Busch on board was a real boost for MLL. Once they were signed up, we wound up getting a couple of other major sponsors, including Merrill Lynch. In fact, we exceeded our projections for sponsors before we even had a single team in place.

Anheuser-Busch was the big one, though. They truly were the Sports Legitimizer. I believed we now had more than enough rope to go out and lasso some big-time owners. I left St. Louis feeling on top of the world.

Back at Anheuser-Busch headquarters, Steve and Kathy felt pretty great about our deal, too. They agreed to back us because they thought lacrosse was cool, and they thought it would attract the young consumers they were looking for. They felt we had a great—and realistic—business model. But most of all, they believed in Dave and me.

Even so, they had seen plenty of new sports leagues crash and burn before a single game was even played. So in the back of their minds, they had one little lingering concern about us: *Will Major League Lacrosse even make it to Season One?*

○

After striking out with a whole bunch of big-money investors, Dave and I changed our strategy. Instead of trying to find another founding partner to join us at the top, we decided to focus on owner-operators who would manage the teams and each invest a seven-figure amount. That would give us enough money to fund the league for at least the first two seasons. We felt it was important to have plenty of cash on reserve, to cover whatever crazy expenses happened to pop up—like, I don't know, $30,000 lights?

Our goal was to start with six to eight teams. And when it came to owners, our strategy, as it's always been, was to go after the best people we could find. I've always worked with the top guys in their fields, like Tim Robertson and Frank Vuono, and I wanted to find that level of owner for our league.

At a cocktail party in Manhattan thrown by Anheuser-Busch, our executive director, Gabby Roe, ran into David Stern, commissioner of the NBA. David loved the idea of our league and gave us just one piece of advice: find the highest quality owners possible, and don't start the league until you have them. That had always been our way of thinking anyway, so that's what we set out to do.

But we realized pretty quickly that the big boys didn't want to play in our sandbox. We contacted top-tier NFL owners like Lamar Hunt, and most of them were really intrigued by the idea of pro outdoor lacrosse. But they wanted to wait and see if it worked before they got involved. They were savvy businessmen who needed to know whatever they invested in was going to be around for a while.

Next, we went after guys who owned minor-league baseball, soccer, and hockey teams. That, we figured, was our sweet spot. They had resources, they had stadiums, and they knew how to run a team. So they became the new objects of our affection.

Yet even as we were meeting with them, we were getting approached by another class of potential owners: the lacrosse enthusiasts. These were really successful guys with a true passion for the sport who were part of the lacrosse community in some way. We were contacted by several groups in several cities who had heard about the league through the lacrosse grapevine and were trying to put together a syndicate of investors so that they could buy a team.

For instance, we heard from a couple of guys in Baltimore who wanted in on the action. One of them, Chris Hutchins, owned Bacharach-Rasin, one of the oldest and biggest lacrosse equipment companies in the U.S. at the time. The other, Ray Schulmeyer, was a veterinarian. They were buddies who both played the sport in college and teamed up to start their own lacrosse tournament for kids in the Maryland area. Chris knew Dave Morrow through Warrior, and heard about MLL from him.

One day, he called Ray while Ray was out raking leaves in his yard. "What do you think about us buying a team?" Chris asked.

"You're nuts," Ray said.

But the more they talked about it, the more they liked the idea. Chris and Ray put together a group of small investors, and they were always on our radar as potential owners.

Another die-hard lacrosse lover came out of Boston. His name was Matt Dwyer, and he fell for the sport after picking up a wooden lacrosse stick in high school; he loved it so much that he carried his stick with him everywhere he went. Matt played a little at Dartmouth and went on to start his own youth league. At his 25th college reunion, he wrote this in the guest book: "I've been very involved with lacrosse, and I hope to get even more involved."

Not much later, he read an article about us in a lacrosse publication, and the lightbulb went on. That night, he turned to his wife in bed and said, "Meg, there's these guys who are starting a pro lacrosse league, and—"

She cut him off with, "Oh, no, here we go again."

The next day, Matt called Gabby Roe and asked about our league. At the time, Boston wasn't part of our game plan—we didn't think the area was ready for pro lacrosse just yet—but Matt seemed to be a very passionate guy, so we told him we'd stay in touch and keep him updated on developments.

Then we hit the road, looking for owners. All in all, I'd say we met with around 75 different groups. Many were made up of smart and savvy entrepreneurs, but a lot of them were just plain wacky. I mean, some of them gave Dave and me reason to fear for the future of humankind. But we weeded out the weirdos and built a list of prospective owners.

Finally, with only a few weeks to go before our official First Draft Day in January 2001, we shrank the list down to six candidates. Initially, we'd wanted to have as many as eight teams, but the truth was we only had six good groups. As much as we would have liked to have an array of suitable candidates to choose from, we just didn't. We felt the smartest thing to do was to start the season with six teams, and, if everything went well, we could expand in Season Two. And so, we picked our Gang of Six.

We found minor-league baseball guys to run a team in Bridgeport, Connecticut.

We got guys with experience in minor-league soccer to handle the team in Rochester.

We decided to go with Chris and Ray to run a team in Baltimore.

We had a fairly solid investment group that wanted a team in New Jersey.

We had a somewhat less solid group in Philadelphia.

And we had a team in Long Island that was going to be owned by our old pal from SoBe, Bill Bishop.

After SoBe sponsored our Summer Showcase, we went back and asked them if they'd be interested in owning their own team. They said no—but Bill, who was leaving the company at that time, said he wanted to buy a team himself. The Bishop family negotiated with SoBe and got the right to use a lizard logo similar to SoBe's, and to call the team the Long Island Lizards. Bill didn't get involved with MLL to make a killing. He got involved because he loved lacrosse, and because he figured owning a team would be fun.

In theory, it was.

What *wasn't* fun was getting all our prospective owners together in one room.

That was a horror show.

You see, individually, all of our ownership groups weren't that hard to deal with. But once they got together, either over the phone or in person, they just didn't get along. Some of these investors had never run a sports team before, and they were skeptical about each other. They were constantly sizing each other up. We kept telling everyone, "Look, guys, we're all in this together. The league is only as strong as our weakest team." But our six groups just never got it together.

So we had a lot of endless conference calls with 35 guys barking back and forth about a million different things. I mean, it was madness! A one-hour call would turn into a four-hour marathon of arguments and accusations. These guys were always threatening to drop out over something or other, and we never really knew from week to week who was in and who was out. We did our best to keep everyone pumped up and generate some momentum, but most of those calls just killed any momentum we had. Personally, I'd never seen anything like this in the years I'd been in business. We simply couldn't get the six groups to work together as one unit.

Dave and I started to wonder if they would ever get along well enough to make the league work, or if this endless arguing would tear us all apart. Let me tell you, those phone calls were some of the shakiest times we had. I honestly didn't know what would happen next.

Then, in November 2000, we invited all the groups to attend a player combine in Florida. With our official Draft Day just a few weeks out, we were going to find out soon enough if our Gang of Six could co-exist.

○

The combine was a two-day event held at the ESPN Wide World of Sports Complex at Disney World in Orlando. We had 164 lacrosse players from around the world show up to strut their stuff. We had a kid who came all the way from South Australia, and a young goalie from Osaka, Japan.

On Saturday, the first day of the combine, the players were out on the field from 8:15 A.M. to 4:15 P.M., running drills, getting timed for speed, and basically showing off their athletic abilities. That evening they took their physicals, and the next day they were back on the field for more drills. We had some top-notch talent evaluators on hand, including Bob Carpenter, publisher of *Inside Lacrosse* magazine and a supporter of the league since day one; Chad Watson, a former All-American midfielder at UNC and an MLL Advisory Team member; and Ted Garber, former head coach at the University of Massachusetts and one of our coaches during the Summer Showcase.

For Sunday evening, we planned a dinner for our potential owners at Pacino's Italian Ristorante in nearby Kissimmee. This would then lead to our big owner-operator meeting the following morning.

Representatives from all of our big six markets showed up at the combine—Bridgeport, Baltimore, New Jersey, Long Island, Rochester, and Philadelphia. We even invited Matt Dwyer from Boston, although we still weren't thinking of him as a serious candidate for Season One.

And we had another guest—a very successful investor who was thinking about launching a team in Washington, D.C. The Big Dog, as we'll call him, would have been a great addition to the league, but he still needed a lot of persuading before he made any kind of commitment. We really needed the combine to run like clockwork so the Big Dog would be impressed and agree to jump on board.

The first two days of the combine went great. The players were amazing, and the feeling on the sidelines was electric. I got so fired up I actually jumped out on the field and led the players through a push-up drill. I could see all the potential owners buzzing with enthusiasm. It was great to get them out of conference rooms and onto a playing field, where they could meet the athletes and get a feel for what owning a team would be like. We wrapped up the combine on a high note, and got ready for our party at Pacino's.

The idea behind the event was for everyone to relax and have fun, and go into the meeting the next day feeling positive.

The dinner itself was a blast—great food, plenty of drinks, good conversation. All our groups were getting along just fine. But at the end of the evening, as everyone was filing out, our executive director, Gabby, stood by the exit and handed out a revised operator agreement to each of the groups.

He might as well have handed out sticks of dynamite.

○

The next morning, we started the operator meeting at eight o'clock in the Disney complex, in the Field House conference room overlooking a beautiful baseball diamond. Tim and Dave and I were there, hoping our Gang of Six could keep it together. You see, the Big Dog wasn't only checking out the players—he was checking out the other potential owners. He had to decide if these were the kinds of guys he wanted to be in business with. So we had to make sure that the meeting didn't deteriorate into yet another shouting match.

I felt we needed some divine intervention, so I asked Tim to say a little prayer for the group before we got started.

Tim got up and quoted the Old Testament, Zechariah 4:10: "Do not despise these small beginnings, for the Lord rejoices to see the work begin."

Amen, Brother.

Then all hell broke loose.

The problem was the revised operator agreement. You see, Gabby's job was to keep our shaky coalition together, and he was understandably worried about all the fighting among the potential owners. He felt that by clarifying what we expected from each group, we could do away with all the bickering. So at the last minute, he changed some of the language and rewrote some of the terms in the operator agreement we'd been using for weeks.

His heart was in the right place, but the timing wasn't great.

Basically, we gave the groups only 12 hours to look over the agreement before our meeting the next day. The new terms completely whacked everybody out. Their reaction, not surprisingly, was, "What are you guys trying to pull?"

What's more, the new agreement knocked us back to square one. Yes, we had spent weeks fighting about our financial model, but at least everyone was arguing about the same things. Now we had introduced a whole new array of things to argue about. The revisions were intended to smooth things over, but they wound up backfiring on us.

The meeting quickly deteriorated into another shouting match. We sat there hashing out all sorts of issues with no direction and no end in sight. To be honest, I couldn't really blame these guys for reacting the way they did. They were handed a document and told to digest it late on a Sunday in time for a Monday-morning meeting. I did my best to listen to everyone and address their concerns and keep them calm, but it was no use. The meeting was slipping out of our control.

Then the Big Dog got up and spoke. His suggestion for cutting through all the clutter was to have every owner put in *twice* as much as what we were asking for.

The Big Dog was used to dealing with major investors with deep pockets, so for him the only way to guarantee the owners' commitment was to have them put in even more money than was needed. Of course, putting up that much money was no big deal for him. But for the other potential owners, it *was* a big deal—and basically a deal breaker. So the Big Dog's idea got shot down pretty quickly.

Then everyone went back to yelling. I looked over at the Big Dog, and he looked over at me. He didn't say anything, but he didn't have to. He just slowly shook his head. We called a short break, and the Big Dog got up and walked out of the room.

We never saw him again.

You know, I guess I can't say that I was surprised.

Don't get me wrong, most of our potential owners were super guys. They were smart and decent businessmen who truly loved lacrosse. But, when it came to the business of sports, we all had a *lot* to learn.

After the Big Dog left, the arguing continued. The meeting ended with nothing accomplished. We left Florida feeling something between concern and utter hopelessness. You see, losing the Big Dog meant we had absolutely no margin for error. We could no longer afford to have one of our six groups drop out. We had to find a way to pull them together—and convince them to finally sign contracts and invest in the league.

The stark reality was that, with just a few weeks to go before Draft Day, we still had no teams, no owners, no nothing. And time was running out.

We scheduled another meeting for December in New York City. That meeting would be the real moment of truth for Major League Lacrosse. Either we could get our guys to come together, or we might have to scrap everything and start over—which meant the league might never happen at all.

Everything was riding on that meeting in New York City.

And what happened there made the Florida conference look like a fun day at Disney World.

○ ○ ○

As you may have figured out, I like to give nicknames to just about everybody. CEOs, celebrities, athletes, the room-service guy—everyone I come in contact with gets a nickname. Even my best pal, Dave Morrow, was usually "Doctor" in our conversations, for no other reason than I liked to loosen him up. It's just my way of having a little fun and getting everyone to relax.

Which brings me to one of our potential owners, whom we shall refer to only by his nickname: the Dude.

The Dude was the guy who was heading up a Philadelphia group of investors. He was born into money, and only later did we discover that he had to get his family's permission to make any kind of investment in our league. Still, he constantly bragged about the stable of racehorses he owned. After a while, some of our guys got tired of hearing about his horses, and started thinking this guy was full of doody. So he became Dood, which became the Dude. I know, not very creative, but you still like it, don't you?

When he came into the picture around the time of the Summer Showcase, we took him at face value and believed he could put together a quality ownership team in Philadelphia. But as the weeks wore on, we started to wish he'd stuck to racing horses.

Basically, the Dude had a problem with our financial model. He didn't agree that we needed to raise enough money to finance the league for two seasons. He believed that paying for one season was good enough. We explained that we simply wanted to make sure the league was a class act, but he felt we were trying to shake him down.

It would be one thing if the Dude had kept his concerns to himself. But he was constantly riling up the other candidates and making life miserable for us at meetings. His whole purpose in life was to find some way to put *less* money into the league, and to convince the other guys to do the same. So we spent a lot of time defending our financial model and fighting off some nutty ideas to cut costs.

For instance, some of the potential owners suggested that we save money by not paying our players.

"Whoa, wait a minute," I said during one crazy meeting. "You don't want to pay the players? What are you guys, nuts?"

They weren't kidding—they were dead serious. "Come on, Jake," they said, "these guys'll play for free." They truly believed it was possible to start a professional sports league and have the athletes "volunteer" their services.

Let me tell you, Dave and I went ballistic over that idea. Dave had been a world-class lacrosse player, and he understood how much sweat and blood it took to get that good. Besides, most of the players were his friends. He had personally convinced them to play in our league, and he'd put his reputation on the line. And now the owners wanted us to say, "Hey, by the way, remember how we talked about you guys getting regular paychecks? Well, scratch that—you're getting nothing"?

Even if we could convince these world-class athletes to play for free, why would we want to? We wanted them to feel like they were part of a professional operation and not some Thursday-night beer league. Dave and I held firm when it came to player salaries, and we won that fight.

But the Dude and the other potential owner-operators kept trying to find ways to whittle down their investment in the league. Never mind that we had already invested our own money, along with hundreds and hundreds of hours of sweat equity. The Gang of Six was basically discounting everything we'd done so far, and asking us to swallow even more of the cost of starting the league.

These discussions went back and forth for several weeks after the combine. We were coming up on the end of 2000, and we still didn't have any kind of serious commitment from any of the Gang of Six. And Draft Day was right around the corner on January 12, 2001. You see, our goal all along had been to start league play in June, and have the season run through the summer.

Some people felt that MLL should launch in the spring to coincide with the college lacrosse season, which is traditionally the sport's most popular time. But we didn't want to have to compete with the start of Major League Baseball in April or the NBA play-offs in May, and we certainly didn't want to go up against the NFL and college football in the fall. Getting a TV deal if we were going head-to-head against those big-time sports would have been impossible—and I was adamant that we needed TV to be considered major league. So we looked for a window that gave us the best chance to land a television deal, and the summer made perfect sense.

Yet in order to play our first game in June, we would have to start getting ready and selling season tickets at least five months ahead of time—which meant we had to have our draft on January 12 and not a day later. Any delays might cause us to have to push back the start of league play another whole year, which would mean losing all the momentum we'd gained from the Summer Showcase. So it was now or never in terms of getting our potential owners on board. We had less wiggle room than ten clowns in a car.

Still, we hoped we could solidify our shaky alliance at our next big meeting in New York City.

That's when we got blindsided by the Dude.

○

We booked a big conference room in the Fifth Avenue offices of SFX, the sports marketing agency in Manhattan. A crisp December chill was in the air as we all made our way to the meeting. Dave and I were optimistic, mainly because Gabby had been reassuring us that the potential owners were on the verge of committing. Still, we worked out two different sets of hand signals with Gabby. If things were going well, he would give us a signal that meant we should move the group toward making solid commitments. But if Gabby sensed that things were going sideways, he'd give us the other signal, which meant we should pull back.

Hey, the only hand signals I wanted to give were six high fives.

We all settled into the plush conference room and kicked off the meeting. We had five ownership groups that were fairly solid—but by no means committed—and one other group (the Dude's Philly group) that was a major question mark. The problem was we had no leeway. After the Big Dog dropped out, we couldn't afford to lose even one of the Gang of Six. We needed all of them, even the Dude, to make the league work. Everything was riding on the next two hours.

I said a few words to get things going and opened the floor for questions.

That's when the Dude stood up.

Dave and I immediately noticed that he looked kind of nervous. He was clearing his throat and shuffling around and unfolding a piece of paper. What was this, the Gettysburg Address?

In fact, the Dude had prepared a speech declaring World War III.

As he started reading his prepared text, Dave and I braced for the worst. It turned out that the Dude had been calling the other owners behind our backs and rallying them to his way of thinking. We thought we were just a few handshakes away from signing up all our owners. Instead, the Dude had undermined all the fragile progress we'd made in the last few weeks and dumped us right back at square one. He wanted to rip up the agreement we'd been working on for months and start all over with his own model.

Our shaky alliance of owners wasn't even an alliance anymore—it was every man for himself, and all of them against us.

I was sitting at that table watching my dream slip away.

I looked over at Dave, and he was just shaking his head in disbelief. I'll give him the honor of recounting what happened next:

We really thought that meeting was going to be where we finalized our group of owners. We had no idea that the Dude was going to get up and sabotage everything, but there he was, giving his little speech. I looked over at Jake, and Jake was just rolling his eyes. Then I looked at Gabby. He was sweating and tugging on his collar like he suddenly couldn't breathe. Everything was falling apart right in front of us.

All of a sudden I see Gabby furiously giving Jake the bad-news signal. And Jake looks at him as if to say, "Yeah, no kidding."

Honestly, I couldn't believe this was happening. There were a lot of moments over the last two years where it looked like we might be done. There were a lot of walls that it looked like we couldn't get over. But we always found some way to keep moving forward. That was Jake's whole thing: don't quit. But now, if we lost this group of owners, we were really screwed. I sat there thinking we might have finally hit the wall we couldn't get over.

That's when Jake spoke up.

He said, "Fellas, this isn't any way to start a business. You all understand the number we came up with, and we've gotten this far agreeing to that number, so you can't just decide on a lower number at the last minute. If you don't put money in now, you'll just have to put it in later. This is what we need to make the league work."

The other owners just sort of sat there, saying nothing. I think they were kind of afraid to stand up to Jake, and that's why they let the Dude do all the talking. But it was also obvious they weren't going to change their minds. The Dude had gotten to them. Our seven-figure investment number looked like it was out the window.

I half expected Jake to pull an Incredible Hulk and flip over the conference table. I mean, these guys had no idea how hard Jake had worked to get us all to this point, and here they were basically throwing out his whole plan.

I wouldn't have blamed him for going off on these guys and really creaming them.

Instead, Jake played it cool. He didn't lose his temper. He didn't even raise his voice. He was passionate and direct, but he kept his emotions in check and just tried to talk everyone onto the same page. It was amazing to see his reaction to the Dude's speech. He was every bit as shocked and angry as I was, but you couldn't tell by looking at him. When things were at their craziest, that's when Jake was at his coolest.

Look, I knew all about playing under pressure from my lacrosse days. But in sports, the way to be successful at crunch time is to not think too much. It's to let your instincts take over and stay loose. In the business world, though, you always have to be thinking—you always have to stay one step ahead of everyone else. So you can't let your emotions get in the way of making good decisions.

That's exactly what Jake was doing in that meeting. The league was hanging by a thread, and he could have just thrown everyone out of the room and started looking for new owners. But he knew that would cost us at least one year, and maybe more. So he stayed calm and he worked his way through the crisis. It was another lesson for me, about how to handle myself in pressure situations in the boardroom. And there would come a time, in the not too distant future, where that lesson would really pay off for me, and for Major League Lacrosse.

Not every owner in that room agreed with the Dude. I remember Ken Paul, who was part of the Bridgeport group, standing up and speaking in our defense. He said that the deal was a fair one, and the owners shouldn't discount all the work the founders had already done. Ken is a terrific guy, and he helped keep the Gang of Six together for the moment, even if it was on the edge of a very steep cliff.

Still, we all left that meeting feeling pretty despondent. Our league was in serious jeopardy. If we had a few months, we might have been able to work out all the problems we had with our potential owners. But we didn't have a few months—we had less than two weeks to Draft Day.

That meeting in Manhattan was probably the closest we came to seeing the whole business collapse.

The following day, I got a call from Gabby. We went over everything that happened and figured out where we stood. Gabby laid out a few options for us to consider.

"Jake, we have a couple of good minor-league baseball and soccer owners, we have three groups of lacrosse enthusiasts, and we have this rogue guy in Philly," he said. "If we go forward now, we're really rolling the dice. We don't know what kind of partners these guys will be. So our options are to take a chance with them, or to fold up shop and take a year off and start over then."

It took me less than two seconds to respond.

"Well, we're not folding up shop, so throw that out," I said. "Look, I know we didn't get Lamar Hunt yet, but we got some good guys here. And anyway, we're not betting on these potential owners. We're not even betting on ourselves. We're betting on lacrosse. So let's put our faith in lacrosse, and let's roll the dice."

That was that. We were not going to fold up shop.

At the same time, we couldn't go forward with the Gang of Six—not with the Dude constantly undermining us. We couldn't start a league with just five teams, either. And we couldn't hope to start a brand-new search and find another owner in just two weeks. So what were we going to do?

Whatever we did, we had to do it immediately. The clock had basically run out. The curtain was dropping. The fat lady was all done singing and getting ready for bed.

Luckily, we had one card to play—one card and one card only. But it was a good one, and it just might work.

We had the Boston guys.

○

The ownership group led by Matt Dwyer was never in our initial plans. We figured that if things went well in the first season, we might expand and field a team in Boston in our second. Matt was incredibly passionate about the league, though, and he kept pushing us to be one of the original teams. So we stayed in touch and kept him in the loop, even while we focused on the Gang of Six.

But now, the Dude had backed us into a corner. We could either accept his demands or see our alliance of owners break apart. Our only hope was to somehow get rid of the Dude, keep the other five owners in place, and bring in the Boston group to create a new Gang of Six. Tricky, but not impossible. Ordinarily, a maneuver like that would take weeks of negotiations to pull off.

We had 24 hours.

Gabby called the Dude and told him to hold tight while we discussed his ideas. Then Gabby called Matt Dwyer in Boston and told him about our plan. Matt was thrilled with the opportunity, but he had a few hard questions. He was a savvy businessman, and he wanted to be sure he was getting in bed with people who knew what they were doing. As Matt and I talked on the phone, the fate of our league hung in the balance.

Basically, Matt took me through some of the numbers in our business plan. He wanted me to justify projected attendance figures and stuff like that. I could have given him the hard sell, but something told me not to. I knew we had a great product, and I knew he was a smart guy, so I figured, *Let me give it to him straight.*

"Listen, Matt," I told him, "you know anyone could write any number they want on a piece of paper. But in the end, you just have to believe in Dave and me. And you have to be sure it's the right thing for you. I don't want to pressure you into anything. It's a big decision, and it's a lot of dough. So if you're gonna do this, you have to do it because you believe in professional outdoor lacrosse."

That was it. That was my whole pitch. If Matt said no, we were going to lose a year—and maybe have to scrap the league altogether. But the last thing we needed was another investor who didn't really want to invest.

After our talk, Gabby called Matt again and told him that if he was in, we needed him to fax a letter of intent immediately. Gabby sat in his home in Berkeley Heights, New Jersey, waiting for his fax machine to come to life.

For a long time, that little machine just sat there, dead silent. Finally, it shot out a single piece of paper.

Matt Dwyer and his Boston group were in.

○

The next call was the easiest one to make. Gabby phoned the Dude and told him his Hail Mary pass had come up short.

"Your model isn't right for us," Gabby said. "We're going in another direction."

With the Dude gone, it was time to repair the damage he had caused. In the end, we agreed to slightly lower our seven-figure investment number to keep the groups happy. Fortunately, we'd done a little better than expected in signing up sponsors, so we could temporarily make up the shortfall. Even with that, our finances would be tight as a drum. It wasn't the way we wanted to go, but we believed we had to do whatever we could to launch the league that summer, and not wait another year. We were afraid that if we put the brakes on now, we might never get started again. So while lowering our investment number wasn't ideal for us, it's what we had to do to keep moving forward.

The good news was that our new Gang of Six, featuring Matt and the Boston boys, was back in business. We had verbal commitments from all of them to invest in the league—but we still didn't have a single signed contract, much less a check, from any of the groups. And there was still a pretty high level of mistrust among them. There were always rumors that one or another of the groups was on the verge of dropping out, so no one wanted to be the first to put in their money. When Draft Day arrived on January 12, 2001, we still hadn't collected a dime from anyone.

We went forward anyway.

The draft was held in Philadelphia, and it went great. We had decided long ago to take the top players in the world and assign them to different teams, rather than making them part of the draft. We wanted to spread the talent out as evenly as we could—and to place as many players in their hometowns as possible. So we did that, and then held the draft for the rest of the athletes and for new players from college. All the groups had their scouting reports and happily filled out their rosters.

I kept a little log of all my meetings back in those days, and on the day of the draft, I wrote the words: "We did it. History was made."

We now had six complete professional lacrosse teams raring to go . . . but we still didn't have a single signed contract.

We also had another big deadline coming up: our debut press conference on March 8 in New York City. That would be our big coming-out party, when we finally announced the start date of our league and introduced all six of our teams. We'd bust out the new uniforms and logos, show off some of our star players, and get everyone all psyched up to see some pro lacrosse. We were planning a major media spectacle! So to be ready for that, we needed to have more than just verbal agreements from our guys.

We needed to know from each one of them if they were in or out. And we needed to know it *yesterday*.

That's when Gabby called and told me that two of the owners were short on cash.

Here we go again.

Are you having fun yet—at my expense?

I was at my house in Los Angeles on a beautiful sunny morning. I went into my home office and closed the door behind me. I sat at my desk and looked out the window at the gently swaying palm trees. I remember everything seemed so peaceful that morning.

But my guts were in a knot. I knew the fate of our league would be decided in the next hour.

On the desk in front of me was a piece of paper. On it were written the names of the six point guys for our groups, and their phone numbers. I took a deep breath, picked up the phone, and called our potential owners one after the other.

And, one by one, I asked them a simple question: "Are you in or out?"

Matt Dwyer and the Boston boys were first. They said they were in. They may have been the last group to come on board, but theirs was the first bank check we received.

Then it was New Jersey's turn. They were in, too.

Then Baltimore. Another go.

Then Long Island. Four out of four.

Then I was on the phone with the Bridgeport group, who told me they were short $100,000.

I told them I'd get back to them.

Next, I called the Rochester group. They were short *$300,000*.

Just like the Bridgeport guy, our Rochester point person told me his group was really excited about the league. He said the experience during Summer Showcase really got them fired up, and they tried as hard as they could to raise the money, but, unfortunately, this was the best they could do in this short amount of time. I thanked him and told him I'd get right back to him.

Then I sat at my desk and thought about my options. I thought about how this whole adventure had started two and a half years earlier, when I happened to read an article about a kid named Dave Morrow. I thought about how I called him out of the blue—Dialing for Dollars—and barely got him to believe it wasn't a prank call.

I thought about how I had plucked Dave out of his comfortable life in Detroit and thrown him to the lions in Hollywood. I thought about how I convinced him to hand over every last nickel he had. I remembered how excited I was about starting the league, and how my excitement got Dave excited, and how Dave and Tim and I agreed to chase our dream in that little coffee shop in Baltimore.

I thought about that handshake agreement I made with Dave at the very beginning. The one where we said, "No matter what happens, as long as we have each other's backs, we'll be okay. No matter what."

It occurred to me as I sat at my desk that *this* was the "no matter what" moment.

I picked up the phone and dialed our Bridgeport guy. "I'll cover the $100,000," I told him.

Then I called the Rochester guy and said, "I'll take on the shortfall."

And then I called Dave and Tim, and told them what I'd done.

"We're good to go," I said. "It's time to roll."

Look, I've done pretty well for myself financially, but that was still a big chunk of change. I have a family, and I always think of them first, so agreeing to help the owners wasn't a decision I took lightly. After I made those calls, I walked into the family room and told my wife I needed to talk to her.

Now, Tracey is the greatest partner any man could hope for, and having her by my side makes me the luckiest guy on the planet. I couldn't have done all the things I've done in my life without her love and support. Still, the last two and a half years had been one crazy misadventure after another. You could hardly blame her for thinking I was off my rocker.

She listened as I told her what I was doing. She thought about it for a moment, then looked me in the eyes and asked, "Do you believe in this league, Jake?"

"You know I do."

"Well then," she said, "I believe in you."

○

We booked a conference room at the swanky Hudson Hotel in New York City on March 8, 2001, to announce the first season of Major League Lacrosse. The last time we held a major press conference, three people from the media showed up.

This time, the room was *packed*. And we made a point not to serve jelly donuts.

It was the biggest press conference the sport of lacrosse had ever seen. Dozens of media members were there. TV cameras positioned around the room caught all the action. All six ownership groups were on hand, with some of their players and big displays featuring their shiny new logos and colors.

We had the Baltimore Bayhawks, and their logo was a fierce hawk with a nasty beak and a killer stare.

We had the Bridgeport Barrage—their logo was a wildly spinning lacrosse ball flying through the air.

The Long Island Lizards' logo featured not one but two green lizards circling each other.

The New Jersey Pride chose a magnificent roaring lion as its mascot.

The Rochester Rattlers featured—you guessed it—a really cool snake coiled around the top of a lacrosse stick.

And the logo of the Boston Cannons was, indeed, a cannon. Matt Dwyer had been surprised to find no team in Boston had ever used the name Cannons, which was a nod to the city's Revolutionary heritage. In fact, aside from the New England Patriots, there weren't any other professional Boston-area sports franchises whose names paid homage to the city's history. Matt was absolutely thrilled with the name—and thrilled to be one of the founding teams.

Like I said, I'm not a suit-and-tie guy, so I showed up at the press conference in a crewneck sweater. Hey, at least I didn't wear my Hawaiian shirt (we were indoors, so who cared if it rained?). Dave wasn't a suit-and-tie guy, either, but I guess he felt he had to clean up his act a little for the press conference. So he wore an olive-green suit —with a dark T-shirt underneath. Dave had his hair slicked back, and he was shuffling around with his hands in his pockets. I asked him how he was doing.

"I'm nervous as hell," he said.

But when it was his turn to speak, Dave went up to the podium, took a deep breath, and knocked it out of the park.

And if his legs were jittery, I didn't notice.

The day of the press conference was an amazing day for all of us. The Gang of Six was over the moon talking about their teams. Players like Casey Powell and Mark Millon were basking in the media attention. And Dave and I were strutting around like a couple of proud peacocks. Very few people in that room knew exactly how hard it had been for us to get to this point. But I knew it, and Dave knew it, and that's what made the moment so much sweeter for us.

We announced the date of our first game—June 7, 2001— between the Baltimore Bayhawks and the Long Island Lizards at Baltimore's Homewood Field.

After the press conference, I did an interview with Charlie Rose for his nightly PBS talk show. You know, just me and him sitting at his famous table in that dark room. When we went on air, he introduced me and got right down to business. Now, Charlie is a pretty serious guy, and he was looking through a *Wall Street Journal* interview I'd just given. He looked up at me and—as if he were grilling a Watergate burglar—asked, "Jake, you are quoted in this article as saying lacrosse is the fastest-growing sport in the country. Do you have any documentation to back that up?"

Documentation? "No, I don't. I just said it."

He looked confused.

"So if you said it, it must be true, right?"

"Yes, Charlie, that's exactly right."

Then the serious Mr. Rose had a big laugh. And so did I.

That's pretty much how I've always handled things. It's like when I told Frank Vuono that Dave's company was worth $27 million. It wasn't that it wasn't true—it just wasn't true *yet*. But I believed it would be someday. If I didn't believe that, I wouldn't have said it.

Remember—the world lets you be what you make them believe you are.

If lacrosse wasn't the country's fastest-growing sport yet, it soon would be, thanks to Major League Lacrosse.

That is—*if* we could make it through our first season.

Plenty of professional leagues had made it to Season One, only to fall apart before they crowned a champion. Getting to the starting line was a major accomplishment for us, but the finish line was still a long way off. Would we beat the odds and make it through the season? Or would we become a cautionary tale for future sports leagues?

We certainly believed we would make it.

But the truth is, there were no guarantees.

12

Back when I was doing the sitcom *Big Brother Jake* on the Family Channel, my wife and I spent a lot of time with Tim Robertson and his family. He had five young, energetic kids who would speed around his home in Virginia Beach. Tracey and I—who didn't have any children of our own yet—would watch those kids run all over the place, and we'd look at each other as if to say, "Wow, we're not ready for this yet."

Well, just about ten years later, our fourth child, Luke, was born. That's right, we have four kids now. And I remember Dave and his wife, Christine—who didn't have kids at that time—hanging around with Tracey and me and our children, and them looking at each other as if to say, "Wow, we're not ready for this yet."

Dave and I had another big day circled on our calendars, and it fell about a month after Luke was born. That day was June 7, 2001—the day of our inaugural Major League Lacrosse game.

Just three weeks before that game, Dave came out to L.A. to shoot the cover of our new lacrosse magazine, which we called *FUEL*. It was going to be packed with photos and stories about our players, so fans could follow the action in the MLL. My friend, the great director and photographer Jay Silverman, agreed to shoot the cover for us. He'd shot some really big stars—Michael Jordan, Magic Johnson, Jackie Chan, you name it—so this was a great opportunity for us to do something special.

Jay came up with this cool idea to feature a Ferrari in the shot. The car would be a symbol of Major League Lacrosse—high-powered, sleek, and super fast. And Dave and I would be working on it in the shop, just as we were working on the league. Jay had a vintage gas pump we used as a prop, and I called my friend Gianluigi Longinotti-Buitoni, president of Ferrari North America, who agreed to send over some Ferrari pit-crew shirts. We showed up at Jay's Los Angeles studio with Michael Watson, one of our top lacrosse players, and Dave and I got decked out in our sporty shirts and dark shades. Mike sat in the car, while I leaned on it and Dave sat next to us. Behind us, the gas pump featured the MLL logo and the words "high octane." The headline: Revved & Ready.

So now we had a great magazine. We had the world's best players ready to go. We had six teams. We had big-time sponsors. We had TV. We had everything you need to launch a pro sports league, except one thing.

Fans.

Here, we faced a serious challenge. For one thing, there had never been a professional outdoor lacrosse league, so the perception was that the best lacrosse was played at the college level. So, the thinking went, why would anyone pay good money to see a pro game when the best of the sport was already available in colleges?

But every college team only has one or maybe two really great players. All of our teams were packed with great players. Every one of our players had been the star of his college team—they all were, quite simply, the best of the best. Major League Lacrosse was exploding with talent, so we knew we had a great product.

We also knew we couldn't get fans to believe that just by telling them. We had to *show* them . . . and to do that, we had to get them to the games.

So we pulled out all the stops in trying to sell tickets for Season One. We were afraid some owners would think that all they had to do was open their doors and count the fans streaming in. But we knew from experience that you had to work around the clock to sell tickets. So we pushed the owners to spend a lot of time collecting data on lacrosse fans, calling warm leads, creating season-ticket plans, and doing whatever they could to pump up interest in MLL.

For instance, Matt Dwyer in Boston hired four kids right out of college to work from 9 A.M. to 8 P.M. doing nothing but making phone calls and pushing tickets to Cannons games. Matt's team worked those kids so hard that three of them quit during the first season. The fourth one may have been chained to his desk for all we know.

Matt and his Boston guys did whatever they could to build an audience—one fan at a time. If they sold a ticket to one kid, they'd ask him who his best buddy was, and didn't he want a ticket, too? If someone told them he was thinking about going to see a game, they wouldn't let him out of their sight until that person actually bought a ticket.

A local lacrosse coach chewed them out for their hard-sell tactics. "You're guilting people into buying tickets," he said.

"We make no apologies," the Boston guys said, "because we know that once we get people to a game, they'll have the time of their lives."

Hey, any start-up business is not for the faint of heart. You've gotta know going in that it's going to be hard, messy work.

So while we knew we had the goods on the field, we were realistic about how many fans we could get in the stands.

Our goal in Season One was to draw around 5,000 fans a game. We were about to find out if that was doable, or if we were flat-out nuts.

○

Our big idea for starting Season One was to have an official opening game in each of our six cities. For the Summer Showcase, we played six games in six weeks, and that was a logistical nightmare.

Now we were playing six games *in ten days.*

The opening game was going to be in Baltimore. The Bayhawks lobbied hard to have it in their city, which had one of the biggest lacrosse fan bases in the country. Plus, the opener would be held at Homewood Field on the campus of Johns Hopkins, one of the most famous lacrosse fields in the country.

Then we matched up the Baltimore Bayhawks and their big star, Mark Millon, with the Long Island Lizards—whose marquee attraction was none other than Casey Powell. We were also officially introducing our two major rule changes: a brand-new shot clock and a two-point arc. So not only were two of our biggest stars going head-to-head, they were playing under a new set of rules guaranteed to create more action on the field. We wanted to make an immediate impression on fans with our new, aggressive style of lacrosse.

We didn't want to just tiptoe into the spotlight. We wanted to blow down the doors and come out firing.

So the opening game would be on a Thursday, followed by our second home opener in Boston on Saturday, then a third opener in New Jersey on Sunday. A couple of days to catch our breath, and then on to the next three openers in Rochester, Long Island, and Bridgeport. Dave and I would attend all six games, which meant that our staff had to plan our schedules down to the minute.

While I didn't expect to have to toss out a PA announcer and call a game myself (though you know I was ready to do that, if it came to it), my role was to do whatever was needed to keep the energy level high. I'd generally come into the city early to do TV, radio, and print interviews. Then, during games, I would run up to the TV booth in the third quarter and add a little color to the commentary. Finally, I would anchor a post-game press conference. At every step, the message was the same: *We've got the fastest-growing sport in the country, we've got the very best players in the world, and we're coming to your town next.*

Oh, and I had one other game-day ritual: watching my favorite channel on TV. Well, yeah, ESPN is my favorite, but that summer I was glued to the Weather Channel.

I can't tell you how many hours I spent staring at meteorological maps of the U.S., praying I wouldn't see those bright green blobs—which meant rain—anywhere near whatever city we were in. Playing on the East Coast in the summer meant that rain was a constant concern for us, and even if we had everything else planned perfectly, a last-minute storm could wash it all away. So I'd sit in my hotel room glued to the Weather Channel. And, just between you and me, sometimes I'd even put on a Hawaiian shirt while I watched.

By this point, those shirts had become an attraction all their own. People in the press would ask, "What kind of Hawaiian shirt is Jake going to wear today?" I even started seeing fans show up to games in them. So Tracey and I went to a thrift shop in Los Angeles and scooped up 30 old Hawaiian shirts. The players had their uniforms, and I had mine.

Finally, it was June 7, the day of our inaugural Major League Lacrosse game. The dream that started with a magazine article more than two-and-a-half years earlier was now on the verge of becoming a reality. I put on one of my finest Hawaiian shirts and made my way to Homewood Field. We were about to make history.

Only one thing was worrying me. The "R" word.

A couple of hours before game time, the sky was a sickening gray. The air felt hot and humid. Rain was a distinct possibility. I went over to Homewood Field and looked up at the stands, where only a handful of fans were sitting. I started pacing, staring up at the clouds and making myself crazy. Was the sky going to open up? Would the threat of rain scare fans away? What if only a hundred people showed up?

I thought of that prayer Tim had said at the combine: "Don't despise small beginnings."

About an hour before the start of the game, Dave and I positioned ourselves near the entrance to Homewood Field and waited, just as we'd done a couple of times during the Summer Showcase. So far, my Hawaiian shirt was working—no rain. At first, small trickles of fans moved from the parking lot into the stadium. Then it went from trickles to clusters.

And then from clusters to waves.

In the end, around 5,000 people turned out.

Dave and I stood near the entrance for quite a while. Yes, it had been amazing to see big crowds turn out for our Summer Showcase. But this was different. This was the *first ever* Major League Lacrosse game. I can't even describe what we were feeling as we watched this mass of people file into Homewood Field. To say we were thrilled doesn't quite do it. I guess we felt a lot of things, all at once— amazement, exhilaration, exhaustion, you name it. But for sure, we both felt an incredible sense of pride and accomplishment.

The day before, there was no such thing as a professional outdoor lacrosse league.

But on this day, there was.

○

Just before game time, we brought out Brian Billick, then head coach of the Baltimore Ravens football team, to handle the ceremonial first face-off. Getting Billick was a major coup for MLL—his Ravens had just won the Super Bowl earlier that year, and he pretty much walked on water in Baltimore. He placed the ball down in between our two face-off guys, posed for a photo, waved to the crowd, then jogged off the field. The place went nuts.

Now it was really showtime. Our inaugural game of Major League Lacrosse was about to begin. I couldn't even hear myself think because the crowd was so loud. After the first shot on goal was taken and went wide right, Bayhawks co-owner Ray Schulmayer had his 13-year-old son, Michael, scamper after the ball. Michael found it and brought it over to his dad.

That ball, the very first ball used by Major League Lacrosse, now sits in a glass case in Ray's house (and, maybe someday, the Smithsonian).

Then, early in the first quarter, the incredible Mark Millon took a pass behind the net, turned quickly, and fired a pass to his teammate Chris Turner just outside the crease. Chris took the shot and scored. Chris will always be remembered for scoring the first goal in Major League Lacrosse history, while Mark is still proud that he had the very first assist.

The game was fantastic. Mark scored a couple of goals, and so did Casey. In the end, the Bayhawks pulled out a win. And afterward, hundreds of fans lined up to meet the players. Our players were incredibly friendly and accessible, handing out hats and signing autographs, and they continued to do that after every single game in Season One.

Tim Robertson, who sponsored a NASCAR team through the Family Channel, always remembered seeing families with young kids coming through the NASCAR garages to meet their favorite drivers, and he knew that kind of interaction was magical—and had helped turn stock-car racing into a top-tier sport.

Now he was seeing the same kind of magic with us.

More than anything, getting through that first game filled us all with a sense of relief. The press was positive, the TV coverage went off without a hitch, and the fans had a blast. Did we break attendance records? No. But like I always say, I count the people in the seats, not the empty seats.

And besides, even if we had only drawn 100 people, that would be 100 more people watching professional outdoor lacrosse than had watched it yesterday.

Don't despise small beginnings . . . onward to Boston!

○

From the moment they came on board after the fiasco with the Dude, our Boston group had been one of our rocks.

Matt Dwyer had put together a really classy ownership group. When he took our business plan to a top venture capitalist he knew to get advice, the guy not only said it looked great but bought in to the team himself. And at one point after Matt had assembled his original group of investors, his general manager, Dave Gross, was approached by a really successful real-estate businessman who begged to invest in the team. Seems the guy had played lacrosse in college back in the 1940s. That's right, the guy was *81 years old.* But he loved lacrosse so much, and was so insistent, that Dave finally called the businessman's sons to make sure the old guy knew what he was doing. They told Dave their dad was just nuts for lacrosse, and he became an investor.

In other words, we never had to worry about the Boston group the way we worried about others. But what we didn't know was how close the Cannons came to having no place to play.

MLL's only rule about stadiums was that they had to seat at least 5,000 fans. Matt Dwyer and his staff called every field and stadium for miles but got nowhere. Boston University and Harvard barely gave them the time of day. His GM, Dave Gross, was running around from field to field, measuring bleachers with his tape measure and always coming up short. Finally, a lacrosse coach told him to check out Cawley Stadium in the city of Lowell.

With the press conference announcing the first game just around the corner, Dave drove out to Lowell late one afternoon just as it was getting dark, hopped the fence, and poked around the empty stadium with a tiny flashlight. It was in a neighborhood that didn't have the best reputation, and the stadium itself was old and quaint. The biggest event they held there was probably the state finals of the Massachusetts Instrumental and Choral Conductors Association. Not exactly Lambeau Field. But Dave Gross saw potential, signed a deal with the city, and spruced the place up for the home opener. Still, he went to bed every night worrying that families wouldn't want to drive out there.

Then, two nights before the home opener, HBO aired a documentary about a boxer from Lowell—and called the area the crack capital of America.

Perfect.

But lo and behold, a great crowd turned out for our game. That's the power of lacrosse.

Matt Dwyer had the cool idea to get an actual cannon and shoot it off every time someone on his team scored a goal. He had a replica of a Revolutionary-era cannon made and shipped to Cawley Stadium. It arrived with just minutes to spare before the game started.

The guy Matt hired to fire the cannon, however, was a no-show.

So Matt went down to the sidelines himself, packed gunpowder in aluminum foil, jammed it into the cannon, and got ready to fire. When one of his guys scored the team's first goal, Matt pulled the igniter, and the cannon went off. The crowd went absolutely bonkers. Matt's ears were ringing for the rest of the game, but he said it was worth it.

Our second home opener also went off without a hitch. Two out of two games with no disasters and great crowds . . . we were building momentum. The Boston game drew a little under 5,000 fans, but they were even more enthusiastic than the Baltimore crowd.

Fans in Baltimore were accustomed to seeing lacrosse, but in Boston —which we always feared might not have a big enough fan base—the thousands of people who showed up rarely got to see great lacrosse action, and they were extra jacked to be able to watch the best of the best.

After the game Dave Gross approached one middle-aged fan and asked him if he had fun.

"No," the guy said, "I didn't."

"How come?" Dave asked.

"Because there was just way too much action."

That was a complaint? Too much action? Too much excitement? Matt and his gang took it as a compliment, and it became the team's unofficial motto: The Boston Cannons—We've Got Too Much Action.

It turned out that the fans in Boston truly loved their lacrosse. Right before the Cannons' second game, a massive storm swept in, and the owners called a lightning delay. Around five thousand fans had already shown up and were now huddled in their cars in the parking lot. Matt and Dave were worried that most of the fans would leave, so they went around from car to car giving people updated weather reports.

But no one left.

That was the moment they realized they had something they could build on.

○

Our third game in New Jersey went great, as did the next three home openers. Those ten days were nonstop craziness. We were always packing up and racing out to the next place, the next interview, the next game. We were lugging around a mountain of swag—huge inflatables, boxes and boxes of hats and shirts, cars decked out with MLL logos. We were juggling media appointments, hotel schedules, and last-minute flights. Somehow we pulled it off.

Yet here's the thing—while everything looked nice and smooth on the surface, behind the scenes Major League Lacrosse was in turmoil.

The Gang of Six was up to its old tricks again. Gabby Roe, Dave, and I had daily morning conference calls with everyone, and we tried to keep them focused on the most important topic—selling tickets. But the guys spent hours complaining about referees, blown calls, and player trades. Those conference calls were endless and excruciating.

Our biggest worry was that we would lose one of our teams during the season. There were probably ten different moments during Season One when everything could have fallen apart. Every day there was a new crisis to deal with, a new fire to put out. We'd work hard to resolve one dispute and come up with a fair solution, only to watch it completely unravel for no reason. And then another dispute would pop up.

We started hearing reports that some owners were disappointed by ticket sales and were laying off staff and spending less on marketing. We tried to explain that if you cut back on marketing you'd sell even *fewer* tickets, but these guys didn't want to hear it.

Or they'd complain that we were paying the players too much. We'd already debated that issue to death, but it kept coming up. We also had some owners who wanted to sign up their own local beer sponsors, even though we had an exclusive deal with Bud Light. Partnering with a local beer distributor might have been more lucrative for them in the short run, but it would have been detrimental for the league. We had to constantly remind everyone that what was good for MLL was good for all of them. But no matter how hard Dave, Gabby, and I tried to convince them that we all had to pull together to make the league work, they continued fighting each other and fighting us.

The only escape from the madness was the games themselves. We all buried our differences and worked together to create a great experience for the fans. We wouldn't allow our internal disarray to make us look unprofessional. So no matter how insane things got behind the scenes—and things got pretty insane—we always put our best foot forward on game day.

Around the middle of Season One, we knew we wanted to do something splashy to generate even more excitement about the league. We had a mid-season All-Star game planned for Bridgeport in August, and we were looking to do something in connection with that. But what? What would give us the biggest bang for our buck?

Then we hit on it. We would ring the bell at the New York Stock Exchange.

There was a strong connection between the sport of lacrosse and Wall Street; in fact, dozens of our players worked in finance in the off-season. Plus, ringing the bell would be great publicity for the league. Everyone loved the idea, and now all we had to do was find a way to make it happen. How hard could it be?

Our All-Star game was scheduled for August 2, so we wanted to ring the bell on that day or maybe August 1. Our press guy, Jaye Cavallo, had a connection at the NYSE from when he worked for the Women's Tennis Association, and he got the wheels in motion. He found out they only had one slot open on either of those days: the closing bell on August 1.

But then we were told that MLL wasn't eligible to ring the bell.

Turns out that you need to have the CEO of a publicly traded company with you in order to ring the bell.

No problem. I called my old pal Angel Martinez at Reebok, and he hooked us up with the company's top guy, Paul Fireman. So now we had us a genuine CEO.

At the same time we were setting that up, we were also working on hosting a lacrosse clinic on the street outside the stock exchange. We planned to set up some inflatables and a big net and have Wall Street guys hang out with our players and fire off a few shots. And we could sell tickets for our All-Star game right on the spot. It was all shaping up to be a publicity bonanza . . . until we found out that our CEO wasn't available on Aug. 1.

We kept pushing forward. Time was running out, so I made a few calls. If you want to say that I pleaded with Paul to change his schedule, I guess that would be fair. We needed the guy. If we lost him, we'd probably lose the closing bell.

At the last minute, he graciously changed his schedule.

On August 1, we roped off a section of Broad Street in lower Manhattan and started setting up our street clinic. Meanwhile, I was in Bridgeport, Connecticut, where our owners were holding a charity fund-raiser at the local zoo. They asked me to be there, and I was happy to help. The plan was to attend that event and do a morning radio show, then fly to Manhattan in time to ring the closing bell at 4 P.M. A tight schedule, but we could do it.

Then, in the middle of the radio show that morning, I got a call from one of our guys. Big trouble on Wall Street.

Turns out that people were seeing our Major League Lacrosse logos all over the street clinic and just assumed we were going public. They were calling the stock exchange and asking about buying shares in MLL. In fact, we should have had Reebok signage up, since that was the company whose CEO was technically ringing the bell. Fortunately, Dick Grasso, then chairman and chief executive of the NYSE, is a big-time lacrosse fan and a really nice guy, and he was kind enough to let our street clinic keep going—provided we put up some Reebok signage.

So one of our guys rushed over to Reebok's Manhattan office and scooped up as many signs and banners as he could carry, then rushed back down to Wall Street and saved the clinic.

Does this kind of stuff happen to the NFL?

Finally, I finished with the radio show and the zoo event in Bridgeport, and got into a helicopter for the ride to Manhattan. We made it with a couple of hours to spare. I put on a suit— the NYSE doesn't allow Hawaiian shirts—and drove down to the stock exchange. I joined Paul, Dick, and a couple of our players on the elevated platform to ring the bell, while the rest of our staff was down on the trading floor. At four o'clock, I put my hands on a big button and pushed down. The closing bell clanged, and everyone cheered.

Now, normally you're supposed to ring the bell for about five seconds. But I kept ringing that sucker for at least ten seconds longer. Finally, Dick Grasso leaned in and whispered to me, "That's enough, Big Shot, get your hands off the bell."

Hey, come on, this was my one big moment on Wall Street, and I wanted to make it last.

○

During Season One, my family and I rented a house in East Hampton, New York. It was a nice place and a reasonable distance from all our game sites. One of the easiest trips I had to make was taking a ferry across Long Island Sound to Bridgeport, where the Barrage played. They held their games in a beautiful place called Bluefish Stadium, by the harbor, and the ferry docked right in front of it.

I enjoyed those ferry rides; in fact, what I really liked doing was bringing my kids up and hanging out with the captain while he steered us to shore. One day, I was up there with the captain pulling into the dock by Bridgeport Bluefish Stadium. One of the Barrage's principle owners, Ken Paul, was waiting for me at the dock. As the ferry pulled in, Ken looked up and saw me next to the captain, and it looked to him like I was steering the ferry.

Ken thought to himself, *That son of a gun Jake has taken over the boat.*

I may not have been steering the ferry, but I did have my hands on the wheel of Major League Lacrosse—and let me tell you, it was some mighty rough sailing. Dave and I did everything we could to keep the league together, but we always felt like we were on the verge of having it all collapse. We spent so much time jumping from one crisis to the next that we could never take a moment and plan for the future. We were always just one step ahead of disaster.

When Dave flew out to East Hampton to stay with us for a few days, he thought he was coming out for a vacation. Instead, we spent hours and hours on conference calls dealing with all kinds of problems. My family would be running to the beach or going for ice cream, while Dave and I could never leave the house. We really solidified our friendship in those crazy times.

Here's how Dave puts it:

> Those first couple of years, Jake always took me with him just about everywhere he went. I was his lacrosse guy, and he always wanted me there to talk up the game. Like I've said before, I wasn't used to going to so many meetings. It was all new to me. The funny thing is, we had a few charts and graphs that our guys had made up for us, but Jake and I never used them in meetings. We never did a PowerPoint presentation or anything like that. It was all shucking and jiving. It was Jake just talking and talking

and talking, delivering this rapid-fire mix of truth and fiction. And somehow, it all made sense.

Almost every meeting we took was about one thing, and it wasn't lacrosse. It was passion. That's what we were selling—passion, passion, passion.

So it was amazing for me to see how deals got done at this level. It was even more amazing for me to watch Jake in action. He was always so sure of himself, always so focused and determined. I sat there at several meetings and events and marveled at how little I knew about what was going on—and at how much Jake knew.

It took me a long, long time to figure it out, but all along I was mistaking Jake's confidence for competence—and I mean that in the nicest possible way. He was always so confident in the way he approached things, and I just assumed he had done all this before. It never dawned on me that Jake was nearly as out of his element and wading in deep waters as I was. Until one day, when he turned to me and said, "Wow, I can't believe how much I've learned since we started."

That's when it suddenly made sense to me.

It wasn't that Jake knew what he was doing—in fact, he was winging it, just like me. It's that he was absolutely fearless about jumping into something and figuring it out as he went. I did that to some degree with Warrior, but Jake showed me that as long as you don't let fear and apprehension slow you down, you can overcome any obstacle, no matter how big or scary it is. That may sound like a cliché, but it's a cliché for a reason—because it's true. The key is being passionate, learning as you go, and moving forward no matter what.

That was a whole new approach to life for me, but being around Jake, I saw that it really works.

Even with our league up and running, Dave and I couldn't stop looking for new investors.

Through our connections we heard about this one guy who'd made a fortune in the cable-television business. We also heard that he loved lacrosse. He lived a mile away from where we were staying in East Hampton, so we made a plan to meet him and ask him to invest. We figured, hey, what did we have to lose—the worst he could do was toss us out. Besides, we were pretty sure we'd already met our quota of colorful, eccentric characters.

Boy, were we wrong.

13

Not long after the All-Star game, Dave and I drove out to see the cable-TV big shot at his home in East Hampton, and pulled into the driveway of a mansion that looked like Count Dracula lived there.

We'd been told that this guy had recently sold his cable business and made a fortune. We were also told that he was a little "different." Over the last few years, Dave and I had met a lot of "different" personalities, so we knew we were in for a pretty interesting meeting. We just didn't know *how* interesting.

We rang the bell, and an older man came out to greet us. He looked like the Christopher Lloyd character in *Back to the Future.* Crazy white hair, tattered khaki pants, and an old Oxford shirt with a frayed collar and sleeves.

"Hi, I'm Double G," he said. "Come on in."

Honestly, this guy looked more like a trespasser than a tycoon. But we weren't there to judge—we were there to make a deal.

Double G offered to take us on a tour of his mansion. What he should have said is, "Let's go on a bar hop." Turns out he had minibar setups everywhere, with a bottle of Scotch and an ice bucket waiting in every room. Dave and I followed cautiously as Double G drank himself from room to room.

Then he started yelling out for his son. I mean, he was hollering this kid's name as loud as he could, but the boy just wouldn't come out. We figured he had to be four or five years old and too shy to join us. Finally, after this guy screamed himself silly, his son made an appearance. He was actually 15 years old and about as tall as we were. He wasn't shy; he was just hiding out from his wacko dad.

We couldn't blame him.

After a long tour and several shots of Scotch (for him, not us), we settled down to talk business. Dave and I appealed to Double G's love of lacrosse and talked about how great our games had been. He seemed interested, and finally asked, "So how much money are we talking about?" Then he took another slug of Scotch and offered us one. We declined for the fifth time.

As aggressive as Dave and I had always been in trying to find investors, the truth is we'd become a little gun-shy. We had so many meetings that went nowhere, and we were tired of going down dead ends. Still, we knew this was a long shot, and we didn't have much to lose. So I took a deep breath and told him what we were looking for.

"Two million dollars," I said.

We expected the guy to gag on his Chivas, or at least have his security guys toss us into the driveway.

Instead, he picked up a yellow legal pad and started making calculations. While we just sat there in silence, he continued drinking and writing on the pad—and hiding what he was writing like a kid taking a math test. Dave and I looked at each other as if to say, "What in the world is going on?" But the guy just kept on doing his calculations.

Finally, after a couple of minutes that felt like a couple of hours, Double G looked up from his yellow legal pad.

"Yes," he said, "I think that number sounds good."

Then he turned the yellow pad around and showed us what he had written. He had circled the number $2,000,000, and underneath drawn a smiley face.

Dave and I were shocked. Almost everybody had thrown us out on our ears, and we hadn't asked them for anywhere near that much.

We were so taken aback we didn't even think to ask Double G for a check then and there. We just got up and shook hands and slapped each other on the back—and, yes, finally took him up on his offer of a drink (which, by the way, tasted like gasoline). Hey, we were celebrating our new $2-million, legal-pad partnership. We agreed to call him after championship weekend and finalize the deal. We thanked Double G profusely and left the mansion clutching the yellow legal pad like it was the Holy Grail.

When we got into my car, all Dave and I could do was sit there, wondering, *What just happened?* We had a legal pad with "$2,000,000" and a smiley face. In some countries that might be considered a binding document. But, last time we checked, not in the USA.

○

We got to the end of Season One with no teams dropping out. That was a major victory for us. None of our teams were backed by big corporations, so we knew that there wasn't a bottomless well of funds for our owner-operators to dip into. Most of the teams got by on sheer hustle and hard work. Ray Schulmayer's wife, for instance, washed all the jerseys and did all the accounting for his squad in Baltimore.

Once the season was over, it was time for the play-offs. Four out of the six teams would square off in two semifinal games, followed by our first championship game. And all of this would take place over Labor Day weekend. That's right, we chose one of the busiest holiday weekends to hold our championships. We figured it would help us make the biggest splash. That was either genius or lunacy—but, hey, you've always got to think big.

Next, we had to figure out where to hold the championships. We considered all of our cities, and even a neutral site, before settling on Bridgeport, Connecticut. There was only one problem.

We had no place to play.

In big sports leagues like the NFL, they know where they're going to play the Super Bowl five years in advance. At Major League Lacrosse, we didn't have that luxury. We announced our first season in March, in order to capitalize on the momentum of the Summer Showcase, and we launched just two months later. We really felt that if we didn't go then, we might never have gone at all. But we launched without having all, or even most, of our ducks in a row. So we knew going in that Season One would be a mad scramble.

Toward the end of the season, after we picked Bridgeport as our championship site, we learned the stadium used by the Bridgeport Barrage wasn't available on Labor Day weekend. So Gabby Roe and our guys started a frantic last-minute search for a venue. Just under the wire, they found the 12,000-seat John F. Kennedy Stadium in Bridgeport. It was a nice, quaint stadium with a lot of things going for it.

Except location.

There are stadiums in this great country of ours that overlook beautiful cities, or oceans, or palm trees. JFK Stadium, however, overlooked the Bridgeport Correctional Center.

That's right, we were playing our first Major League Lacrosse championship game right next to a prison. Not the most family-friendly choice, I guess.

I remember Dave Morrow walking up the path that led to the stadium with a bunch of fans, and seeing people stepping around something on the ground. He looked down and saw a freshly dead squirrel 20 feet from the entrance. Hey, that's classy. Then he heard a kid asking his dad, "Are those prisoners?" Sure enough, a row of inmates had a bird's-eye, end-zone view of the stadium.

Dave turned to Ray Schulmayer and said, "A prison? We're playing next to a prison?" Not surprisingly, Ray had no comment.

But I guess it was fitting, considering everything we'd been through. It seemed we just weren't going to do anything by the book.

Still, we drew a good crowd, and after two thrilling semifinal games, only two teams were standing: the Baltimore Bayhawks and the Long Island Lizards. A rematch of our opening game—and yet another epic battle between Casey Powell and Mark Millon. We couldn't have asked for much more drama for our title game.

In fact, the 2001 Long Island Lizards may have been one the greatest lacrosse teams ever assembled in the sport's history.

Besides Casey Powell, probably the best offensive player of his generation, they had both of the legendary Gait brothers, Paul and Gary, who played brilliantly all season. The Lizards also had Terry Riordan, a four-time All-American and the leading all-time scorer at lacrosse powerhouse Johns Hopkins. And they had Sal LoCascio, one of the greatest goalies in history and a three-time gold-medal winner in the World Championships.

Bill Bishop and his Long Island crew believed that this was, person for person, the best lacrosse team of all time. And you know, it would be pretty hard to argue.

That was the point of our league, though. We always put the very best players in the world on a field and let them go at it. Before the season, we heard from a million people who told us our experiment would fail. They said the rule changes would ruin the sport, and the games wouldn't be half as exciting as a college matchup. The purists just didn't want to believe we had a shot.

By the end of the season, however, many of them had changed their minds. Guys like Richie Moran, a Hall of Fame player who went on to coach Cornell University's lacrosse team for 29 years and win three national championships in a seven-year span. Richie was about as old school as old school gets. Then Ray Schulmayer invited him to a Bayhawks–Lizards game.

Richie watched world-class players like Gary Gait and Casey Powell fly up and down the field, and he turned to Ray and said, "This is the way lacrosse used to be played. This is the way it *should* be played."

Just before the finals, Governor John Rowland declared Labor Day weekend to be "Major League Lacrosse weekend" in the state of Connecticut. In the championship game, Casey Powell played beautifully. It was great to see how, in just one season, he had grown into a real team leader. In the end, Powell and the Gait brothers led the Lizards to a 15–11 win. Afterward, Dave and I presented Bill Bishop with the Steinfeld championship trophy. (That's right, the trophy is named after me. Our TV announcer, Quint Kessenich, called it the "Steinfeld Cup" on the air and later asked me what I thought of that. I said,

"What do you think I think? I love it!" Hey, wouldn't you like to have a trophy named after you?)

When we handed off that trophy, I don't know who felt better, Bill or us.

There were so many moments when it looked like Major League Lacrosse would fall apart, yet here we were, presenting our championship trophy after a successful Season One. Overall, our attendance was pretty good for a league that said *go* just four months earlier. Most important, we'd finished what we had started—we got through Season One.

Yet no sooner had we presented that trophy than we had to confront a really unpleasant reality.

Major League Lacrosse was out of money.

○

You have to understand, our goal was never to get through just one season. Our goal was always to create a league that would be around for a long, long time. So while surviving Season One was cause for celebration, we didn't waste a lot of time patting ourselves on the back.

Instead, we got right to work, figuring out how to have a Season Two.

We sat down and looked at all the positives first. For one thing, we had successfully launched a league, and that isn't an easy thing to do. So many leagues don't have the infrastructure to survive even one season. But we felt we had a solid structure in place.

On top of that, we were beginning to launch the brand of Major League Lacrosse, and our brand stood for something: the best players, the fastest game, the most exciting action. And our players were more than just amazing athletes—they became, as we had hoped, ambassadors for the game. They showed up early and stayed late, and they signed every single autograph.

In other words, we felt we had a good foundation that we could build on. It's like I've always said whenever someone asked me how the league was doing: "Every day we're alive, we get a little bit stronger."

Onward and upward to Season Two, right? Not so fast.

Financially, Major League Lacrosse was always on a tightrope. Our initial plan to have enough breathing room to last two seasons never happened, so we knew going in we were setting ourselves up for problems down the line. Most start-ups run into all kinds of unexpected expenses, and that's why we fought so hard to have a contingency fund. But in the end, we had no contingency fund.

What's more, our owners didn't have deep pockets—and they wouldn't stop fighting with each other. So we always had to live with the possibility that one or more of the teams would drop out of the league.

Even so, we never had a single conversation about shutting down after Season One. Everyone at MLL just assumed we'd have a Season Two. We didn't know exactly how we'd pull it off. But not for a moment did any of us think we wouldn't.

Were we in denial? Maybe. But we still had our insurance policy: Double G and his Picasso-like doodlings on that legal pad.

The first thing we did was set up a conference call with the owner-operators. Basically, it was time to ask for more funds from the group. We had told them if they didn't come up with our seven-figure investment number before the season started, they would have to come up with it eventually—and eventually was now. So we braced ourselves for another crazy conference call, and we got everyone on the line.

I explained the situation: we were out of money. We needed everyone to re-up so we could give ourselves a shot for a second season. I thought I got through to the group, but when I asked team by team who's in and who's not, the only team that was willing to keep going was Boston.

I took a deep breath, knowing that Tim, Dave, and I needed to talk before we made our next move. I asked everyone to think about it overnight, and told them we should all get back on the phone early the next morning.

So that meant the make-or-break moment for Major League Lacrosse was scheduled for 10 A.M. on September 11, 2001.

○

Many of our MLL guys, including Gabby Roe and Dave Klewan, were in our offices in Secaucus, New Jersey, early that morning. They were calling sponsors and handling other league business. Our offices were on a high floor, and had a clear view of downtown Manhattan. All of a sudden, someone noticed smoke coming out of one of the World Trade Center towers. Everyone went over to the window to look . . . only to see a plane hit the other tower.

They stood there watching in disbelief as both towers collapsed.

Everyone thought about our players. So many of our guys worked on Wall Street during the off-season—as many as 40 percent. We had no way of knowing how many of them worked in the towers or nearby. Just like everyone else in the tri-state area, we started making phone calls, trying to find the people we cared about.

Thankfully, we didn't lose any players. But the tragedy of 9/11, which stopped the world in its tracks, stopped Major League Lacrosse, too.

In the days that followed, we truly didn't know what was going to happen to the league. We didn't know if the owners would bail, or even if the U.S. economy would collapse. No one was thinking about lacrosse, or even about business—they were thinking about their families. No one wanted to talk to us about the future of the league.

Eventually, Dave and I did get our six groups back on the phone. We told them again that the league was out of money. But we also said that we understood what a difficult situation everyone was in.

"This is an insane time for the world," I said. "So if you want to get out, you can absolutely get out. No one would think badly of anyone if they did."

Except for the Boston group, they all said they were ready to close up shop.

We told everyone to sit tight, and that we would call them all back soon.

We'd also had a phone call set up with our old pal Double G for September 11. Obviously, it didn't happen. When I called him a few days later, he didn't pick up. I called him a bunch of times during the next week and left him messages, but he never returned them. Finally, he called back.

"I've moved my family into a bomb shelter," Double G told me. "I can't tell you where we are. America is under siege. Everything is falling apart. I'm afraid I can't give you any money. Farewell."

And that was that. We never heard from Double G again.

○

I called Dave in Detroit and Tim in Virginia Beach, and the three of us mulled over our options and considered our next step. No one would have blamed us if, in the face of all that uncertainty, we simply shut down the league and went away. People would say, "You guys gave it a great try, but who expected something like 9/11 to happen?" The truth was, we had a hard enough time making a go of it when the economy was booming and the country was at peace. But suddenly, the world was upside down. What chance did we have now?

So it all boiled down to that phone call with Dave and Tim and me. We had survived so many last-gasp moments when the league could have collapsed, but there had never been a more obvious time to cut our losses and walk away.

We were as close as we'd ever been to making Major League Lacrosse a footnote.

"Look, guys," I finally said, "we could close this thing down and say we took our shot and just walk away. No one would blame us if we shut down now. I mean, with everything that's gone wrong, we shouldn't even be here today. There's no logical reason we're still in existence.

"But you know what?" I continued, "We've come this far, and we've gone through so much, that I believe we have something here. So I don't know about you guys, but I want to keep it going."

I waited for Dave and Tim to respond.

"I'm in," Dave said.

"Me, too," Tim said.

Our plan was simple: the three of us would keep doing what we'd been doing. Dave would keep working the lacrosse side, and Tim and I would put enough funds in to keep things going for a while. It wasn't an easy decision to make, but the long and short of it was that we just didn't want to see our dream end this way.

We didn't want to be only a footnote.

We got back on the phone with all the owners and sponsors and told them we were still in business. Then we went to work doing what we did every day from Day One—finding a way to make it happen.

I remember just recently opening the little datebook I kept in those early days, and seeing a note I made on the page for October 16, 2001. I didn't write much. In fact, it was all of eight letters. But it spoke volumes.

What I wrote was, "MLL Lives."

Not long ago I was watching my son Luke play in a youth-league soccer match. Remember I told you about Luke, who was born just a month before our first Major League Lacrosse game in 2001? Well, as I write this, he is 11 years old, and he's a great, tough little guy. He loves all sports, including soccer and, yes, lacrosse.

So I was standing on the sidelines watching him play, alongside my friend Sugar Ray Leonard, whose son also played on the team. Ray is one of the greatest champions in the history of boxing, and pound for pound maybe the best fighter of all time. I mean, the guy won world titles in five different weight classes. But on that day we were just two dads watching our boys play soccer.

"Hey Jake," Ray said to me, "that little guy out there, No. 11, is that your son?"

"Yep, that's Lukey."

Ray looked over and said, "You know what? That little guy has got heart. And you can't teach heart."

You can't teach heart.

That made me feel great, coming from a guy like Ray Leonard, who has a heart the size of California.

In essence, it also summarizes the story you've just read. Because if the creation of Major League Lacrosse was about anything, it was about heart.

It wasn't about business decisions or market research or investment options. It wasn't about pie charts or PowerPoint presentations or cross-promotional strategies. It was about tenacity, courage, and going with your gut. It was about not listening when everyone told us we should quit. It was about a simple handshake agreement between two new friends.

It was about heart. And it still is.

As you read this, Major League Lacrosse is just about to wrap up its 12th season, and we're finishing stronger than ever. We've added two new teams: one in Charlotte, North Carolina; and one in Columbus, Ohio. Our plan is to double the size of the league—from 8 teams to 16—by 2019. And we're expanding our TV partnerships all the time.

How did we make it this far, considering how bleak things looked in the weeks and months after 9/11?

It wasn't easy.

The fact is, the American economy was down in the dumps in the years after 9/11, and we found ourselves trying to keep the league afloat in the middle of a really bad recession. Finding new sponsors or investors was all but impossible. For a long time, we had to continue to fund the league ourselves. The first few seasons of Major League Lacrosse were always touch and go.

Yet two things kept us going: our belief that we had a truly great product, and the hope that we would find good people to get involved with us.

I always believed that I'd be the one to find the right person or the right group to step in and finally put Major League Lacrosse on solid ground. But in the end, it wasn't me or any of my connections who stepped up.

It was my great pal Dave Morrow.

○

Did I tell you about the first time I put Dave through one of my workouts? It happened not long after I first phoned him way back in the spring of 1998. He met me at the gym in L.A., and I put him through my usual high-rep exercises.

Dave told me he felt like his heart was going to burst through his chest. Still, he pushed his way through to the end.

The next day, when Dave got on a plane, he said his muscles were so sore that he couldn't lift his arms over his head. He couldn't even scratch his nose. So when he tried to lift his roller suitcase and put it in the overhead bin, he barely got it off the ground. The passengers assumed he had some kind of physical disability. Finally, a petite flight attendant came over and lifted Dave's bag for him.

Hey, it happens to the best of them, even world-class athletes like Dave.

My point in telling the story, though, is this: Dave is one tough cookie.

You can't always tell from hanging out with him, because he's quiet, casual, and laid-back. But Dave has never given less than 150 percent of himself, and he's always had my back no matter what— just like he promised he would. Dave never quit.

I couldn't have asked for a tougher guy to go into battle with.

Dave's role in MLL had always been to handle the lacrosse side of things, but I recognized something else in him from the very start. I saw that, despite his low-key demeanor, he was someone who got things done. And in the course of launching Major League Lacrosse, I introduced him to all sorts of people and put him in all kinds of situations, and all that prepared him for the biggest meeting of his life.

When we joined forces, Dave's company, Warrior, was small but growing. In its first few years, it didn't come close to reaching a million dollars in sales. But Dave was smart enough to realize that helping me create a pro lacrosse league would only help Warrior grow.

That's exactly what happened.

Let me back up the story a bit—back to our second season. Warrior was growing bigger and bigger, and one day Dave got a call from a sales rep, Jim Teatom, who told Dave that his boss wanted to meet him.

"Who's your boss?" Dave asked.

"Jim Davis."

Jim Davis is the chairman of New Balance, one of the biggest sports-footwear companies in the world. But Dave didn't know all that much about Jim or New Balance, and guessed that the company might earn $100 million or so a year.

Then Jim Teatom explained New Balance has annual revenues of $1.5 billion. Dave took the meeting.

Let's let him take you through what happened next:

I flew to meet Jim Davis at the New Balance corporate headquarters in Boston. It was a 12-story building with the giant NB logo on top. I felt a little intimidated just walking into this place. Then I went up to a conference room and saw Jim and several executives waiting for me around a big table. Now I felt even more intimidated.

Jim asked me about Warrior, and talked a little about New Balance. The vibe was friendly, and I finally relaxed. Maybe I relaxed too much. "You know," I blurted out, "I came here thinking you guys would be big-shot jerks, but you're all right."

Everyone laughed. The ice was broken. Then Jim got down to business.

"Dave, the reason we invited you here," he said, "is we want to buy your company."

I sat there in stunned silence while a dozen executives tried to read my body language. What my body was saying was, "Huh?"

Honestly, the thought that they wanted to buy Warrior never once crossed my mind. And I never thought about selling it until that moment. They caught me so off guard that I hemmed and hawed and said something like, "That is really cool, but, gosh, it's not for sale."

Jim said, "Everything is for sale."

I explained that I felt Warrior was just getting started, that I had a lot of unfinished business and really wasn't interested in selling it. What Jim said next really surprised me.

"I like you," he told me, "and I want to help you out. What can I do to help you out?"

I didn't hesitate.

"Well," I said, "Jake Steinfeld and I started Major League Lacrosse, and we're looking to raise more money. Maybe you can help with that."

"Send me the numbers and we'll look them over," he said.

New Balance wound up not only buying a major stake in Major League Lacrosse, but also developing a new lacrosse cleat and becoming our footwear sponsor.

That, by itself, was a great, great thing, and it allowed MLL to close its funding gaps. But that wasn't the end of my involvement with Jim Davis.

Over the next year or so, he kept asking me about Warrior, and I kept telling him it wasn't for sale. Finally, he invited me to see him again. He'd heard that I'd been approached by a couple of other equipment companies, and that I'd even taken a meeting or two. He basically said that if I was going to sell Warrior, I absolutely had to give him first crack. I was really given the full-court press in that meeting.

I left completely unsure of what to do. I had discussed selling Warrior with my wife, Christine, and we both thought it was something we could do if the price was right. But now that I had to make a decision, I felt really confused.

So I called Jake. I told him all about the meeting and asked for his advice.

"Do you want to sell your company, buddy?" he asked.

"If the price is right, yeah," I said.

"Do you have a number in mind?"

"Yeah, I have a number. But I haven't done any valuations or a market plan or—"

Jake cut me off. "If you have a number in mind, and you think it's a fair number, then Jim will think it's fair, too. Tell him the number, and he'll do it."

That's it? Just come up with a number and blurt it out? I repeated that we hadn't combed our books and run the numbers and come up with an official valuation. Jake cut me off again.

"Cancel your plane ticket home, call his secretary, and set up an appointment. Then go in there and get it knocked out."

Only Jake can make selling your company sound as simple as folding your laundry.

After I got off the phone, I called one of my best friends from college, Billy Frist. Billy and his wife, Jennifer, were the ones who made a crucial early investment in Warrior that allowed us to grow. I told Billy that I was thinking about going in to see Jim Davis without an offering memorandum or any other paperwork.

"What are you, crazy?" Billy said. "They will laugh at you."

"Maybe," I said, "but it just feels right."

I cancelled my plane ticket and called Jim's secretary to make an appointment. In the cab ride over to New Balance headquarters, my heart was pounding so hard I thought I was going to pass out. I went to the elevators and pressed the up button, then felt so nervous that I walked away. I was halfway out of the building when I stopped and walked back. I felt light-headed and nauseated. I couldn't believe I was doing this. But I sucked it up and went upstairs.

"So what's so important you had to see me this quickly?" Jim asked.

"I've been thinking," I said. "I need the right financial partner, and I feel you guys are the right ones. Let's make it happen." Then I just blurted out my number.

Jim thought about it for a moment and said, "That sounds reasonable."

We came to terms right there in his office—and just 90 days later, I sold Warrior to Jim and New Balance. For exactly the number I asked for.

Looking back, I can't believe I had the confidence to walk into Jim's office and negotiate that deal. Just a couple of years earlier, I would have walked out of that lobby and never come back. Heck, I wouldn't have even been there in the first place. But now I was developing this new confidence. I was starting to believe in myself more than ever. And somehow I summoned the courage to go in there and get my number.

To this day, I refer to that as my Jake moment.

Storming into meetings without lawyers and accountants is exactly the kind of thing Jake does all the time. I went to so many meetings with him where he just got up and won people over with passion and persistence, and I guess his way of thinking just seeped into my brain. He also taught me that the key to a good business deal is to make it fair for both sides. Jake never took advantage of anyone, ever. He was always, *always* respectful of the other side. I mean, the guy is sweet and polite to receptionists and waiters and basically everybody. I never once saw Jake big-time anyone.

In that way, he taught me about the power of relationships. Jake's whole life has been about relationships and friendships. He always says he's a really rich man, not because he has money but because he has so many great friends. So when I had this amazing opportunity in front of me, it made sense to me to make the deal with Jim one-on-one. I would have never dreamed of doing that if I hadn't met Jake.

It turned out to be one of the best decisions of my life.

My deal with Jim Davis was great for both of us, and great for Major League Lacrosse. Maybe it would have happened anyway if I had waited another year or two, but who knows?

What I do know is that I wouldn't have cancelled my plane ticket and gone back to see Jim if I hadn't called Jake.

Jake always says life is about moments.

Well, that was one of those moments.

These days, I have a lot of Jake moments. I've grown so much since joining forces with him. I'm proud to still be the CEO of Warrior nine years after my deal with New Balance. We're one of the fastest-growing sporting-goods brands in the world, with hundreds of millions of dollars in sales in over 75 countries. I've also had the great fortune to become good friends with Jim, who gave me the opportunity and the mentoring I needed to build Warrior into the global brand it is today.

And, of course, I'm thrilled to still be involved with Major League Lacrosse. MLL is fortunate to have a partner like Jim Davis—without his leadership and continued financial support year in and year out, MLL would not be here today. I believe that, together, Jim, Jake, and I are going to see the league get even bigger and better.

Looking back on it all, it's been a crazy, amazing ride, and there were a lot of really scary moments along the way. But I never stopped having Jake's back, and he never stopped having mine.

That handshake deal is still in effect. It's all we've ever needed.

The way my pal handled his deal with Jim Davis makes me feel really proud. When I met him, Dave was a brilliant young guy with a passion for lacrosse and some great ideas for its future. Working with him to launch the league, we both went through so many crazy things and survived so many insane setbacks. I watched Dave become more confident with every weird meeting and every disaster averted. Today, he's an incredible man, and I'm proud to call him one of my very best friends.

Oh, and remember how back in 2001 Dave and his wife weren't ready for children of their own? Well, they've got four kids now—Samantha, Kevin, Jessica, and Maximus.

○

Dave's deal with Jim gave us a huge shot in the arm, and allowed us to grow the league even more. But that doesn't mean all the craziness was over.

As Major League Lacrosse grew and got stronger, we got more and more excited about the idea of expanding, and in 2006, we added four new teams—in Denver, Chicago, San Francisco, and Los Angeles. The L.A. team, in particular, was a big deal for me, since I had long wanted to put a team in the city where I live.

Unfortunately, the expansion didn't work out. For various reasons—including management challenges, venue issues, and a recession—four of our teams folded by the end of the 2008 season. Did that hurt? Of course it did. Was it a setback? You know it. It was only temporary, though. We felt we had to retract and regroup, so we could live to fight another day. Hey, things get nuts sometimes, not only in business but in life. But like I always say, success is failure turned inside out.

You know what? Looking back on it all now, I have nothing but good thoughts and proud memories of every moment along the way—and of every person who took this amazing ride with us. The original players, the guys in the front office, and the Gang of Six—they all played a part in the creation of Major League Lacrosse because they all believed in this crazy dream when nobody else did. And, quite frankly, they are the *only* ones who can say, "Hey, I was there at the beginning, when this remarkable league was born." That makes them all pioneers. And for that, I thank them, from the bottom of my heart.

○

Today, Major League Lacrosse is going strong and getting stronger. We still have a long way to go, though, and many things we still want to accomplish. The experience of watching a lacrosse game in person is out of this world, and we're now working on making the TV experience every bit as thrilling. There are some really awesome technological innovations on our horizon.

In other words, you ain't seen nothing yet.

Since Major League Lacrosse started, we've watched a whole new generation of lacrosse players explode in front of our eyes. So many of those little kids who were lining up to meet Mark and Casey after games in our first season are in college now, and playing the game at a higher level than it ever has been played. Great athletes who ten years ago would have chosen football or baseball are instead choosing lacrosse—so the players are getting bigger, stronger, and faster.

And Major League Lacrosse has had a lot to do with that.

"Not all that long ago, most kids who loved lacrosse only dreamed about playing on a top college team," says Casey Powell. "But today, they dream about playing in the MLL. I know, because I'm around these kids all the time, and that's what they tell me. They say, 'One day, I want to play in the MLL.'"

So that, my friend, is the story of how Major League Lacrosse got started. I hope you had as much fun reading it as we had living it.

I also hope you take some inspiration from our story. I hope you realize that amazing things are possible if you dedicate yourself 110 percent and never quit. Take it from us, there is no dream too crazy or too far-fetched to come true, as long as you believe in that dream with all your heart.

We can't tell you exactly how to make your dream come true. We barely knew how to make *ours* come true.

But we can tell you what you absolutely *have* to do to have any chance of succeeding. You have to get up, get out there, and *take a shot.*

Good luck, and don't forget your Hawaiian shirt!

Don't quit on you!

○ ○ ○

SUMMER SHOWCASE AND SEASON ONE ROSTERS

We'd like to acknowledge all the people and players who helped us make history with Major League Lacrosse, from the Summer Showcase in 2000 all the way through Season One. You will all be remembered forever.

MAJOR LEAGUE LACROSSE
SUMMER SHOWCASE 2000

MLL Staff

Gabby Roe
Dave Klewan
Jaye Cavallo
Meredith Elwell
Jill Haber
John Walsh
Terry Eason

SFX Team Members

Frank Vuono
Peter Hughes
Mike Trager
Bob O'Connor
Bill Allard
Scott Easton
Emilio Collins
Dave Robertson

MLL Summer Showcase 2000: "The 40"

Mike Abeles
Marshall Abrams
Mike Battista
Jake Bergey
Mike Busza
Brian Carcaterra
Greg Cattrano
Roy Colsey
Dave Curry
Ryan Curtis
Dan Denihan
Dudley Dixon
Rob Doerr
Kevin Finneran
Mark Frye
John Gagliardi
Jim Gonnella
John Grant, Jr.
Jamie Hanford
A. J. Haugen
Jon Hess
Jesse Hubbard
Jay Jalbert
Corey Kalhoun

Craig Kalhoun
Dennis Kelly
Brian Kuczma
Sal LoCascio
Mario Lopez
Darren Lowe
Curt Lunkenheimer
Dan Martin
Chris Massey
Drew McKnight
Blake Miller
Mark Millon
Matt Ogelsby
Casey Powell
Ryan Powell
Tucker Radebaugh
Brian Reese
Mike Regan
Josh Sims
Lorne Smith
Tim Soudan
Dave Stilley
Greg Traynor
Brian Voelker
Michael Watson

MAJOR LEAGUE LACROSSE
SEASON ONE 2001
"THE ORIGINAL SIX"

Baltimore Bayhawks

Ownership

Chris Hutchins
Ray Schulmayer
Dave Pivec
Gordon Boone

Brian Voelker, GM and head coach

Players

Adam Borcz	1
Paul Cantabene	5
Greg Cattrano	2
Dan Denihan	47
Dudley Dixon	33
Rob Doerr	6
Hugh Donovan	43
Matt Dwan	7
Mark Frye	24
Kip Fulks	13
Brian Hole	20

Tom Marechek	42
Dan Martin	11
Greg McCavera	12
Tim McGeeney	10
Mark Millon	9
Shawn Nadelen	18
Gavin Prout	8
Brian Reese	34
Matt Shearer	17
Rob Shek	19
Josh Sims	4
Tom Slate	3
Jeff Sonke	15
Jarred Testa	39
Chris Turner	44

Boston Cannons

Ownership

Matt Dwyer
John Brennan
R. William Burgess
John DeSantis
Peter Fahey
Richard Frisbie
Martin Zweig

Dave Gross, GM
Mitch Whiteley, head coach

Players

Mike Abeles	12
Mike Battista	44
Mike Busza	41
Gerry Byrne	33
Kenny Crowley	18
Ryan Curtis	6
Billy Daye	2
Scott Doyle	11
Bill Edell	21
David Evans	16
Mike Henehan	8
David Jenkins	5
Doug Knight	7
Brian Kuczma	43
Mike Law	3
Kurt Lunkenheimer	27
Dan Radebaugh	51
Tucker Radebaugh	17
Benny Strutt	26
Rodney Tapp	38
Andy Towers	29
Greg Traynor	99
Michael Watson	4
Tim Whiteley	14
David Winslow	1

Bridgeport Barrage

Ownership

Ken Paul
Mickey Herbert
Charlie Dowd
Bob Watson

Ken Paul, GM
Ted Garber, head coach

Players

Matt Alexander	10
Joe Brock	13
Tom Carmean	45
Rodger Colbert	18
Roy Colsey	3
Keith Cromwell	16
David Crone	6
Harold Drumm	44
Ken Garcia	11
Jin Gonnella	15
Brian Haggerty	8
Jamie Hanford	5
Nick Hartofilis	12
Scott Hochstadt	24

Dennis Kelly	2
Brian Langtry	1
Mario Lopez	14
Pat McGinnis	18
Blake Miller	26
Jim Mule	21
Tom Naglieri	17
Matt Panetta	22
Jed Raymond	34
Brian Silcott	4
Matt Striebel	23

Long Island Lizards

Ownership

Bill Bishop, Sr.
Bill Bishop, Jr.
Chris Bishop
Joe DeSimone
Mike DeSimone
Ray Suris
George Diffendale

Mike Fox, GM
John DeTommaso, head coach

Players

Joe Astarita	24
Tim Brynes	21
Brian Carcaterra	23
Kevin Finneran	33
John Gagliardi	11
Gary Gait	1
Paul Gait	3
Joe Ghedina	42
Tim Goettelmann	9
A. J. Haugen	12
Steve Huff	44
David Kelly	7
Steve Kisslinger	77
Sal LoCascio	2
Pat McCabe	29
Rob Mulligan	10
Matt O'Kelly	26
Casey Powell	22
Sean Radebaugh	14
Terry Riordan	19
Billy Serino	4
Stephen Sombrotto	25
Vincent Sombrotto	16
Brian Spallina	91
Eric Wedin	5

New Jersey Pride

Ownership

Bob Turco
John Flood

Charlie Shoulberg, GM
Ted Georgalas, head coach

Players

Justin Berry	1
Matt Caione	9
Paul Carcaterra	44
Jason Carrier	2
Joe Ceglla	42
Christian Cook	37
David Curry	15
Patrick Dutton	25
Jon Hess	9
Jesse Hubbard	16
Reid Jackson	40
Peter Jacobs	24
Jay Jalbert	10
Mike Keenan	14
Steve Koudelka	0
Chris Malone	7

Drew Melchionni	23
Todd Minerly	74
Tom Ryan	17
David Stilley	35
Dennis Sullivan	5
Trevor Tierney	6
Rob Torti	12
Scott Urick	30
Jeff Wills	99

Rochester Rattlers

Ownership

Frank DuRoss
Chris Economides
Steve Donner

Jody Gage, GM
Guy Van Arsdale, head coach

Players

Marshall Abrams	43
Ric Beardsley	13
Jake Bergey	66
Steve Bishko	20
Chris Cercy	15
Casey Connor	4
Brian Dougherty	3
John Fay	12
John Grant, Jr.	24
Jeremy Hollenbeck	16
Cory Kahoun	19
Tracey Kelusky	34
Tim Morrissey	8
Adam Platzer	7
Ryan Powell	22
Mike Regan	21
Chris Schiller	2
Tim Soudan	33
D'Arcy Sweet	17
Regy Thorpe	11
Andrew Whipple	1

○ ○ ○

ACKNOWLEDGMENTS

I would like to thank, first and foremost, my partners in this amazing adventure, Dave Morrow and Tim Robertson—you always had my back, and you're like brothers to me.

Thank you also to our publisher, Reid Tracy; our editor, Shannon Littrell; and the whole gang at Hay House, for making this experience so enjoyable.

Thanks, of course, to my literary agents Jan Miller and Shannon Marven at Dupree Miller, who do what they do better than anyone else in the world.

I'd also like to acknowledge Dave Gross, who in my eyes is the most talented commissioner in professional sports. We're lucky to have him. And to my partner with the pen, Alex Tresniowski, thanks for helping me tell this story. Thanks to the guys in the booth and on the sideline, Quint Kessenich, Joe Beninati, Mike Crispino, and my good buddy Brian Kilmeade.

Thanks to Craig Morganti ("C"), my right-hand man; to my attorney and great friend Bob Lieberman, who has been there since the beginning; and to the brilliant producer—and my pal—

Frank Marshall. Oh, and Dave Morrow has a couple to add as well: Bill Tierney, Billy and Jennifer Frist, and Brooke Coburn.

A very heartfelt thank-you to everyone who not only played a part in this story but also helped me recount it in this book, starting with Frank Vuono and Angel Martinez, two of the best and brightest guys I've ever met. Thanks also to Dave Klewan, Gabby Roe, Jaye Cavallo, Heidi Krupp, Jo-Ann Geffen, Rick Allen, Matt Dwyer, Ray Schulmayer, Chris Hutchins, Ken Paul, Ted Garber, Steve Uline, Kathy Casso, Bill Bishop, Bob Carpenter, Casey Powell, Mark Millon, Marty Feldman Eyes, and Bow-Tie Bob.

And a special thanks to everyone at Major League Lacrosse, both past—John Algie, Jason Chandler, Porter Hayes, Mark Kastrud, Mike Lieberman, Shaun May, Susan Petrovic, Eric Rhew, and Rachel Spates—and present—Chris Day, Ryan Guerinot, Aly Morrissey, Kerry Pucillo, Amy Saulen, Ryan Sweeney, and Cassie Watson. You guys have all worked so tirelessly to not only grow our great league, but also the great game of lacrosse.

ABOUT THE AUTHORS

Jake Steinfeld is a world-renowned fitness expert and motivator who founded Major League Lacrosse in 1998. The founder and chairman of Body by Jake Global® LLC, he pioneered the personal-fitness-training industry and created America's first fitness-lifestyle television network, FitTV. He served as chair of the Governors' Council on Physical Fitness and Sports for California, and is presently chair of the National Foundation for Governor's Fitness Councils.

Jake is also the *New York Times* and *Wall Street Journal* best-selling author of *I've Seen a Lot of Famous People Naked, and They've Got Nothing On You!: Business Secrets from the Ultimate Street-Smart Entrepreneur;* as well as *Powerliving by Jake: Eleven Lessons to Change Your Life; Don't Quit!: Motivation and Exercise to Bring Out the Winner in You—One Day at a Time;* and *Get Strong!: Body by Jake's Guide to Building Confidence, Muscles, and a Great Future for Teenage Guys.* Jake lives with his wife, Tracey, and their four children in Los Angeles, California.

Website: **www.bodybyjake.com**

○

Dave Morrow is an entrepreneur, businessman, and co-founder of Major League Lacrosse (MLL). The former star of the Princeton Tigers men's lacrosse team from 1990 to 1993, he was a three-time United States Intercollegiate Lacrosse Association (USILA) All-American, twice making the first team.

In an illustrious college career, Dave still holds the distinction of being the last defenseman to earn the NCAA lacrosse player of the year award, was a two-time NCAA defenseman of the year, and made the all–Ivy League first team three times. During his collegiate career, Princeton won the school's first NCAA tournament championship, won two Ivy League championships, and earned the school's first four NCAA tournament invitations. Following college, he represented Team USA in the 1994 and 1998 World Lacrosse Championships and was named to the 1998 All-World Team.

Dave's equipment company, Warrior Sports, is a leading equipment provider to professional, collegiate, and interscholastic teams and players. It provides a variety of equipment and has propagated the interest in titanium material for use in lacrosse and ice-hockey equipment. By cofounding the MLL, he has expanded professional lacrosse from box lacrosse to field lacrosse. Dave lives with his wife, Christine, and four children in Michigan.

Website: **www.warrior.com**

○ ○ ○

Hay House Titles of Related Interest

YOU CAN HEAL YOUR LIFE, the movie,
starring Louise L. Hay & Friends
(available as a 1-DVD program and an expanded 2-DVD set)
Watch the trailer at: **www.LouiseHayMovie.com**

THE SHIFT, the movie,
starring Dr. Wayne W. Dyer
(available as a 1-DVD program and an expanded 2-DVD set)
Watch the trailer at: **www.DyerMovie.com**

○

*EXCUSES BEGONE!: How to Change Lifelong, Self-Defeating Thinking
Habits,* by Dr. Wayne W. Dyer

*IT'S NOT THE END OF THE WORLD: Developing Resilience in Times
of Change,* by Joan Borysenko, Ph.D.

THE REAL RULES OF LIFE: Balancing Life's Terms with Your Own,
by Ken Druck, Ph.D.

*SUCCESS INTELLIGENCE: Essential Lessons and Practices from the
World's Leading Coaching Program on Authentic Success,*
by Robert Holden, Ph.D.

All of the above are available at your local bookstore,
or may be ordered by contacting Hay House (see next page).

○

We hope you enjoyed this Hay House book. If you'd
like to receive our online catalog featuring additional information
on Hay House books and products, or if you'd like to find
out more about the Hay Foundation, please contact:

Hay House, Inc., P.O. Box 5100, Carlsbad, CA 92018-5100
(760) 431-7695 or (800) 654-5126
(760) 431-6948 (fax) or (800) 650-5115 (fax)
www.hayhouse.com® • **www.hayfoundation.org**

○

Published and distributed in Australia by: Hay House
Australia Pty. Ltd., 18/36 Ralph St., Alexandria NSW 2015
Phone: 612-9669-4299 • *Fax:* 612-9669-4144 • www.hayhouse.com.au

Published and distributed in the United Kingdom by: Hay House UK, Ltd.,
292B Kensal Rd., London W10 5BE • *Phone:* 44-20-8962-1230
Fax: 44-20-8962-1239 • www.hayhouse.co.uk

Published and distributed in the Republic of South Africa by:
Hay House SA (Pty), Ltd., P.O. Box 990, Witkoppen 2068
Phone/Fax: 27-11-467-8904 • www.hayhouse.co.za

Published in India by: Hay House Publishers India, Muskaan Complex,
Plot No. 3, B-2, Vasant Kunj, New Delhi 110 070 • *Phone:* 91-11-4176-1620
Fax: 91-11-4176-1630 • www.hayhouse.co.in

Distributed in Canada by: Raincoast, 9050 Shaughnessy St.,
Vancouver, B.C. V6P 6E5 • *Phone:* (604) 323-7100 • *Fax:* (604) 323-2600
www.raincoast.com

○

Take Your Soul on a Vacation

Visit **www.HealYourLife.com®** to regroup, recharge,
and reconnect with your own magnificence.
Featuring blogs, mind-body-spirit news, and life-changing
wisdom from Louise Hay and friends.

Visit **www.HealYourLife.com** today!